BLUENOSE

THE OCEAN KNOWS HER NAME

HEATHER-ANNE GETSON

NIMBUS
PUBLISHING

D1158562

Nimbus Publishing Limited
PO Box 9166
Halifax, NS B3K 5M8
(902) 455-4286
www.nimbus.ns.ca

Printed and bound in Canada
Design: Min Landry, Wink Design

Photo credits: All photos appear courtesy of Nova Scotia Archives and Record Management except the following: Fort Point Museum, page 6; Kejimkujik National Park, page 2; Maritime Museum of the Atlantic: page 5; Wallace MacAskill, pages 7, 8, 25, 26, 28, 30, 32, 34, 36, 44, 48, 51, 68, 70, 72, 94

Library and Archives Canada Cataloguing in Publication

Getson, Heather Anne
Bluenose : the ocean knows her name / Heather Anne Getson.
ISBN 1-55109-538-6

1. Bluenose (Ship)—History. I. Title.
VM395.B5G48 2006   387.2'2   C2006-900695-4

We acknowledge the financial support of the Government of Canada through the Book Publishing Industry Development Program (BPIDP) and the Canada Council, and of the Province of Nova Scotia through the Department of Tourism, Culture and Heritage for our publishing activities.

Contents

PREVIOUS PAGE: ***Bluenose* Racing Up the Harbour, 1931**. *This W. R. MacAskill photograph skilfully captures the romantic era of the tall schooners during the final years of the sailing bank-fishery. Wallace MacAskill was born in St. Peters, Cape Breton, and grew up on the shores of the Bras d'Or lakes, a sailing Mecca even for children. As an eleven-year-old he had a sailboat of his own to cruise the shoreline and at the age of twelve he received his first camera. Photography and sailing would be his two life-long passions. His marine photographs won hundreds of national and international awards and throughout the life of the* Bluenose, *W. R. MacAskill almost single-handedly recorded the schooner's every race. In 1929, one of his inimitable photos of* Bluenose *was chosen for a 50-cent stamp that was later declared by the New Haven Philatelic Society to be the world's most beautiful engraved stamp. Over 6000 MacAskill negatives survive today and most of the collection centres around the lore and legends of the sea during the decades when* Bluenose *sailed the seas.*

PROLOGUE

"THE OLD GIRL"

The captain roared with the force of a gale, "Keep your heads down!" The shortness of his words belied the measured depths of tone forced into each syllable. Heard from stem to stern, his voice was like thunder filled with the promise of well-aimed bolts of lightning. The rush of wind and salt spray were everywhere, but on the deck of the schooner *Bluenose* the force of nature that demanded total obedience was Captain Angus J. Walters. It was October 26, 1938, and they were in the last race for the cup. The International Fishermen's Series trophy was theirs to defend, and hopefully win, again.

Along the deck the only people who were seen in their entirety were those who had critical roles in the race. They stood near the masts and at the wheel. The remainder of the crew crouched or sat on the deck, not willing to provoke another outburst telling them to keep down. Hatch covers were open to allow air to sail through the vessel. Grown men sat like dutiful children, legs bent or straight before them. Woe to any structure or human that impeded the forward surge of *Bluenose*.

There were extra men aboard the vessel for this one last race. In amongst the born-and-bred Nova Scotians was an American racing enthusiast, Clifford Handy. Every chance that he dared to lift his head was accompanied by the lone, muted eye of his

Bluenose *Racing off Boston, 1938.* *The 1938 International Fishermen's Series was*
Bluenose's *finest hour. In the fifth and final race* Bluenose *averaged a speed of just over*

fourteen knots, one of the fastest speeds ever recorded over a fixed course by a canvassed vessel. Bluenose *is shown here in the first race of the series.*

camera. He knew enough to stay out of the way of Captain Walters and the wind, but wanted yet to record every detail.

Situated near the wheel and partially sheltered by the companionway leading below to the after-cabin, three spirited Canadians broadcast a live radio commentary. It was the first time that *Bluenose* carried a crew of radio reporters, and their job was fraught with double danger. Frank Willis, with a set of headphones clasped to his ears, displayed the agility of a tightrope walker balanced precariously between the need to stand and send regular reports and the need to keep the live broadcasts clear of the language that freely flowed around him, language sometimes as salty as the Atlantic itself.

"The old girl," as they called *Bluenose*, was seventeen years old. Every creak and groan of the hull and every rapid heartbeat of the sails spoke of one last mad attempt to keep the cup from falling into the hands of the challenger, the eight-year-old *Gertrude L. Thebaud*.

The entire month of October had been gobbled up in this best-of-five series. Weather, ageing vessels, and spirited disputes had prolonged the series. Arguments about race details had turned into fierce controversies, and anger had erupted on both sides. In the first race, *Bluenose* had been late getting to the starting line and had had her fore-topmast carried away before finishing three minutes behind *Thebaud*. The second race on October 13 saw *Bluenose* even the score and beat *Thebaud* by twelve minutes. Fog and calm weather then set in causing delays and making both sides anxious and edgy. An American protest claimed that *Bluenose* had swollen around her waist, putting her waterline over the maximum allowable length of 112 feet. This forced Captain Walters to remove ballast to get the ship to ride higher and shorter on the water. But surprisingly *Bluenose* seemed to perform better with less weight. *Bluenose* won the third race by six minutes but lost the fourth, tying the series at two apiece. Whichever vessel won today would be champion forever.

Some of the crew hardly dared to breathe, but everyone was urging *Bluenose* forward, with a united sense of purpose. "Win, *Bluenose*. Win." Someone thought that they heard Captain Angus whisper, "Just one more time, old girl. Just one more time."

The finish line was no more than ten minutes ahead, after a race that saw the two schooners often neck-and-neck. Only ten minutes to go and the whole world would know who had won and who had lost.

In that moment, the crew, captain, and vessel joined as one heaving, breathing entity.

Like a sentient being, the schooner seemed to sense the prize of victory in the air. With a powerful forward surge, *Bluenose* moved well beyond *Gertrude L. Thebaud,* all eyes focused on the finish.

For the thousands of people who lined the shore and wharves of the harbour and for those perched atop vessels at dock, it was a vision from the old days of sail: two finely matched schooners with their black hulls racing to the finish.

Bluenose *Surging in Topsail, 1938.* *This classic W. R. MacAskill photograph was entitled, "All hands and cook." Remarking on that final race between* Bluenose *and* Thebaud *in his last year aboard* Bluenose, *crewmember Claude Darrach wrote, "When the two schooners were closing in on the finish line, there was an awareness of something unusual in the behaviour of the wind, as though it understood that what was happening at the moment would, in future, be remembered as the end of an era."*

Victory Dinner in Honour of Captain Angus Walters, 1938. *This panoramic photograph was taken at the Canadian Club in Boston on November 1, 1938, to honour Captain Walters's last sailing victory aboard* Bluenose. *The win marked the end of the era of the large commercial sailing vessels all over the world. Claude Darrach writes: "The series completed,* Bluenose *loaded the engines, component parts, and the controversial ballast. She sailed home to Lunenburg."*

Then, in a rapid rush of sail and almost three minutes ahead of *Gertrude L. Thebaud*, *Bluenose* crossed the finish line first, for the last time. A hush fell over the waterfront as *Bluenose* dipped and almost curtsied, moving still further into port. Then, in a blaze of celebration and tribute to the Queen of the North Atlantic, every voice, bell, horn, and whistle rose in jubilation. This was not simply a race between two vessels; *Bluenose* and *Gertrude L. Thebaud* had performed on a world-sized stage. People would always remember the courage and skill of fishermen and their schooners.

The diary of Arthur Risser, proprietor of Risser's Restaurant in Lunenburg, captures the sentiments of the people of Lunenburg on this momentous day: "Thursday, November 3, 1938. Fine and warm N.W. wind lovely day. The *Bluenose* arrived home from her race across the sea, Champion of the North Atlantic. She never was beaten in five races for the cup. Looks like this will finish these races. This old Town gave Angus and his crew a great welcome with a big parade and Band. This day will be history for Lunenburg."

There would never be another International Fishermen's Series. It was over. Fast and able large schooners would no longer fish commercially or carry freight. But by the same token, the pride and glow of *Bluenose*'s victory would never die.

THE NORTH ATLANTIC OCEAN

The North Atlantic Ocean is an ancient, shifting entity. The land, perched at the ocean's edge, is surrounded by a mixture of sea air, fog, and the endless wash of waves. Go to the seashore and close your eyes. You can taste, smell, feel, and even hear the mighty Atlantic, soft one moment, unforgiving the next. Open your eyes and the ocean stretches beyond the horizon, unless the coast is swathed in fog, at which point particles of the ocean itself surround and touch you, hazy and full of a salty wetness.

The eastern seaboard of North America is a mass of land that groaned and heaved itself into shape 380 million years ago. Two ancient continents, Laurentia and Gondwana, came together in a massive collision that produced the Appalachian Mountains of eastern North America and much of the land as we know it today.

With the shifting of mighty sections of our planet, the coastline was formed, including the submerged areas that are now commonly called "the banks." Parts of these shallow plateaux were once above sea level, but slowly they've found their place beneath the waves. The fishing banks were well suited by nature as a healthy habitat for fish. With depths of three to four hundred feet below sea level, the mixture of sunlight and nutrients created a perfect balance for many denizens of the deep.

Among the earliest human inhabitants of the present-day Maritimes were the Mi'kmaq. They called themselves L'nu'k, meaning "the people," and lived according to a distinct social and cultural system. Their belief in the Supreme Being and their sense of equality with all living things were hallmarks of their existence prior to the arrival of Europeans. They were hunters and gatherers, spending many months of the year on the coast.

Mi'kmaq With Birch Bark Canoe
For travel along inland waterways First Nations people built light-weight, highly versatile canoes that could carry people and freight through narrow streams, often drawing only a few inches of water. Ocean-going canoes were "hogged" in the middle, like the one pictured here, to allow for some stability against wave and tidal action and to make possible travel between the mainland and the numerous island in Mahone Bay, Lunenburg harbour, and the LaHave River.

L'nu'k may have been the first of Canada's First Nations people to encounter European explorers, adventurers, and fishermen. By the 1600s there was an active trade economy between the two groups. Eventually, the newcomers established permanent settlements.

The creation of European settlements was often driven by political considerations. The settlement of Lunenburg, Nova Scotia, in 1753, is an example of this. Just prior to the Seven Years' War, Great Britain wanted to fill Nova Scotia with hardworking people who would be loyal to the British Crown. Based on the success of the Pennsylvania Dutch (Deutsch) in the 1730s, their fellow landsmen were invited to settle in Nova Scotia. By 1753, the British, who had been collecting these people in Halifax, decided to position all of the so-called "Foreign Protestants"—among whom were Swiss and French Huguenots, in addition to Germans—in one area: a settlement

Lunenburg Harbour circa 1898, with vessels at anchor*. When this photograph was taken in the closing years of the nineteenth century, Lunenburg was a major deep-sea fishing centre with few equals in its dominance of the banks fishery—with the exception of Gloucester, Massachusetts.*

named Lunenburg, in honour of the King of England, who was also the Duke of Brunswick-Lunenburg.

Previously known as Merlegueche, Lunenburg was the second British colonial settlement in Nova Scotia after Halifax, and was the first attempt by British authorities to establish a new civilian colony outside the confines of Halifax harbour. The settlement was put under the military command of Colonel Charles Lawrence and laid out on a neck of land between what became known as the front and back harbours. Each settler received a town lot, a garden lot nearby, and a three-hundred-acre farm lot in the surrounding forest. The town grew steadily to become a bustling south shore community with a mixed farming, lumber, fishing, and shipbuilding economy.

The immigrants who settled Lunenburg were farmers and carpenters, journeymen and apprentices. They were not fishermen or shipbuilders. They were, however, practical. They recognized that their future prosperity was connected to fish and the ocean, rather than to the rock-infested land. By 1760, the first of the Lunenburg-built boats had established steady trade with Halifax and fished the inshore waters.

After Confederation, Lunenburgers began to seriously exploit the Grand Banks fishery with the introduction of trawl fishing from dories. By 1880, nearly all of the two hundred Nova Scotian vessels on the Grand Banks were from Lunenburg. Hundreds of schooners and thousands of fishermen and their families called Lunenburg home. When the vessels were all in port, their masts made the harbour look a like a forest of spars.

Geographically, if not politically, there has always been a north-south connection between eastern seaboard communities. Gloucester, Massachusetts, has a longer history than Lunenburg, with settlement dating back to the 1600s. Filled with ambition, generations of Gloucestermen have fished the banks of the North Atlantic. It was here that a new style of vessel was observed in 1713, with one wise wag commenting, "see how she schoons!" Their schooners were filled with brave men and heaping cargoes of fish. Gloucestermen were known all over the world and they inspired Kipling's immortal Captain Courageous.

There was a fluidity of movement between the fishermen of the East Coast. Newfoundland fishermen came to Nova Scotia, and Nova Scotians often went to the Boston States, meaning Gloucester and Boston. Courage and a spirit of adventure filled the hearts of fishermen everywhere.

People said that the good fortune of Lunenburg "hung on a fish hook," and double dory fishing was the best thing that ever happened to the Lunenburg economy. Called double dory fishing because there were two men in each dory, it was borrowed from the Gloucestermen and began in Lunenburg in 1873. The technology was simple. Each schooner carried eight to twelve dories to the banks. Each dory had miles of trawl line and thousands of fishhooks. If the skipper knew what he was doing, he would find an area rich with cod and the men would begin to fish. Every morning, except Sunday, the dories would leave the schooner and set out a mile or more away from the mother vessel.

The dorymen set long lines of trawl, positioned with anchors and buoys. Thousands of hooks tempted the cod with bits of chopped bait—usually herring. The trawl lines were checked two or three times a day and the fish were taken aboard the schooner. From there, the captain and the rest of the dressing gang would clean the fish and put them in salt, in the hold of the schooner.

Dory Fishing on the Banks, c.1870s. *Lunenburg's Captain Benjamin Anderson began the extremely profitable but dangerous practice of deep-sea trawl fishing from dories, as his schooner* Dylitris *began making regular trips to the Grand Banks. Fishing with multiple baited hooks on a single line from small boats revolutionized the fishing industry with Lunenburg becoming the fishing capital of Canada's east coast.*

Often the youngest member of the crew, sometimes only ten or twelve years old, would help with the dressing down of the fish. The name of each job clearly reflected the duty: header, throater, splitter, and salter. The youngest and most inexperienced member of the crew was called the flunky. The flunky was at the beck and call of the entire crew and was rarely paid a wage.

Lunenburg schooners were built to hold a lot of fish. The success of the fishing trips depended greatly on the hard work of the fishermen and the ability of the captain to find the fish. If the schooner brought in the largest catch of the year, the captain was the Highliner, meaning that his lines of trawl caught the highest number. If he barely went from one season to the next, he was known as a fish peddler. The catches for each trip were carefully reported in the local newspapers. Lists were published for the three trips of the year: the frozen baiting trip, the spring trip, and the summer trip. The latter ended by late September or early October, when numerous schooners would arrive in Lunenburg loaded down with salt cod. Some schooners would then head out to the West Indies to trade fish for rum and sugar, but many would tie up until after Christmas, then head out again for the Grand Banks.

Fish Drying on Flakes, South Shore, 1893. Cod flakes were the long wooden platforms on posts about three feet off the ground where the fish was placed to dry. These flakes were common sights in the towns and villages along the Atlantic coast until the early 1950s.

The work of fishing, as such, did not stop at the end of the summer trip, in September. The dory loads of salt fish were carefully taken ashore and dried by the fish makers. The split fish were placed on fish flakes to dry. The fish (usually cod) had to be turned frequently and at the first sign of rain or fog, the catch would be gathered up and placed under cover. A soft cure was the result of only one or two days' drying and was known as "wet fish." Too much sun would burn the fish; rain could also ruin it. While the fish were on the flakes, men, women and children helped to ensure that the catch would not be spoiled. If the weather was good, three weeks of intense fish making would prepare the product for market. The Lunenburg fish were most often sold to the West Indies. Split, salted, and properly dried, cod can be kept without spoiling for months, even in the warm latitudes of the tropics.

Bluenose *on the stocks at the Smith and Rhuland Shipyard, Lunenburg.* *Smith and Rhuland began by building mainly three-masted tern schooners, but after World War One, two-masted schooners for the fishing and cargo trades were favoured, especially after* Bluenose *proved her worth. Other famous vessels include the rum-runner* I'm Alone *and HMS* Bounty. *In 1963,* Bluenose II *was launched from this famous shipyard.*

However, not every Lunenburger was a fisherman. Lunenburg harbour was rimmed with businesses that helped the fishing industry prosper: there were boatbuilders, block makers, sail lofts, a foundry, and thriving shipyards. Every business hinged on fishing, but not every person went to sea.

Schooners Moored for Winter, Lunenburg Harbour, c.1920. *This Wallace R. MacAskill photograph looks over the front harbour to the tanyard and Kaulback's Head (originally Sutherland's Point), which*

is now the site of the Lunenburg Golf Club. On the far right of this photograph stood the Common Range, ten thirty-acre farm lots that remained inside the town boundary after incorporation in 1888.

Bluenose *Launch, March 26, 1921. A sailing vessel is usually launched before it is fully finished. Spars, rigging, and stepping of the mast are crucial operations that are often left for another day.*

This photograph shows the two-mast Bluenose *just before it slid down the ways and entered Lunenburg harbour. Some local fishermen recalled that she appeared a bit squat without her topmasts.*

This was the world into which Richard Smith and George Rhuland launched Lunenburg's last shipyard in 1900. By that time, over thirteen thousand boats of all sorts had been launched out of Lunenburg. But Smith and Rhuland would become the most renowned of all Lunenburg shipbuilders. Throughout the twentieth century, they would remain the main shipbuilding firm in Lunenburg, taking over from the David Smith and John Bruno yards that had built many of the nineteenth century's ocean-going vessels.

On March 26, 1921, the Smith and Rhuland Shipyard gave birth to its 121st vessel. It was the last Saturday in March and the town had a festive air. Businesses had given their employees a half-day holiday to watch the launch. The new schooner was called *Bluenose*, and hundreds of people crowded the shipyard hill to watch the event. Spectators had journeyed from Halifax by early morning trains. Others had walked for miles through the spring mud, or had driven by ox teams or cars.

Dozens of the more adventurous spectators climbed aboard the new vessel, prior to the launch, and walked on deck, from stem to stern. At 9:45 A.M. the word rang out that only the official guests were allowed to remain on board; everyone else was told to leave the schooner.

The official party included only one woman—nineteen-year-old Audrey Smith. As the daughter of one of the shipbuilders and the niece of the captain, Angus J. Walters, Smith had been asked to christen the new schooner. Somewhat afraid of heights, she appreciated the support of her uncle, John Walters, who helped her climb from the planked walkway to the deck of *Bluenose* and stood with her.

At 10:00 A.M. Audrey Smith went to the bow of Lunenburg's newest schooner, spoke a few words, lowered a bottle of champagne, and broke it on the stem. The spectators cheered and tossed their hats in the air, some of them yelling the familiar Lunenburg cry of "Wedge up and knock down the dogs!" Sledgehammers appeared and struck away the fetters. After a short hesitation, *Bluenose* gracefully slid down the ways and entered Lunenburg's front harbour.

Perhaps the only people who were not filled with absolute delight at the sight of this perfect launch were the members of the local chapter of the Women's Christian Temperance Union (WCTU), who had discussed the launch and other matters of concern at their March 18 meeting. According to the minutes of that meeting,

Mayor William Duff and Miss Audrey Smith at Bluenose Launch. *Lunenburg mayor Duff, who was also MP for Lunenburg County and later appointed to the Senate, is seen here on Zwicker's Wharf. With Mayor Duff is Audrey Smith, who, against the wishes of the WCTU, christened* Bluenose *with a bottle of champagne.*

The President called the attention of the members to the fact that the Magic Baking Powder Company print several recipes in their cook book which call for the use of wine and brandy.

Miss McLeod moved that the manufacturers of this powder be asked to eliminate these objectionable and unlawful recipes from their cook book; Mrs. Iversen seconded the motion and it was passed.

Mrs. Powers asked if any person present knew if the *Bluenose* was to be christened with wine. Mrs. Richard Smith said that wine had not been used for years. The President suggested that we donate a bottle of grape juice and a boquet [*sic*] of flowers. Mrs. Parker suggested that a committee be appointed to collect flowers. Mrs. Hirtle and Mrs. Mason were chosen to get the flowers.

They earnestly asked Captain Walters if this bouquet of flowers, rather than alcohol, could be used to christen the new vessel, in keeping with the spirit and law of prohibition. In a rare moment of silence, history has not recorded Captain Walters's response to the WCTU. Archival film footage of the launch does, however, clearly capture the sparkle and splash of the champagne.

After the launch, *Bluenose* was taken to the Zwicker and Company wharf, to be properly rigged and outfitted. As the crowds of people began to drift away from the shipyard to enjoy what was left of their Saturday, few fully recognized the historic significance of the event that they had just witnessed. A clerk at the Smith and Rhuland Shipyard made a modest and simple entry in the company's log: "Vessel number 121 launched this day. Name: Bluenose."

THE RACING SPIRIT

Lunenburgers say that the sea gets in your blood. It is a statement of truth for fishermen and yachtsmen alike. The thrill of a good vessel and crew, in a race for fish or fortune, is something all Maritimers understand. Poets and businesspeople, royalty and commoners, have all shared this bond.

It was one of the world's greatest yacht races that indirectly spawned *Bluenose*. In 1851, Great Britain's Royal Yacht Squadron was caught up in the general celebrations of Victoria's England and the extraordinary construction of the Crystal Palace as part of the first world's fair, the Great Exhibition. They organized a sixty-mile race around the Isle of Wight, which was held between a fleet of British yachts and an invited guest from the United States, *America*. The vessels were to race for a new trophy called the One Hundred Guineas Cup, which had been purchased and donated by the first Marquess of Anglesey.

Much to the chagrin of the organizers, *America* handily defeated all British entrants and won the race. Queen Victoria, asking about the outcome, was told America had won. She paused and asked who had come in second place. Since the American ship had crossed the finish line while all remaining yachts were still far from sight, the reply was given in ponderous tones: "Madam, there is no second."

America took the cup home to New York, where the trophy's name was changed to the America's Cup and a new set of race regulations was created. It was a defining moment in the history of yacht racing. The America's Cup Series was subsequently held at irregular intervals between yachts representing Great Britain and the United States. Despite valiant attempts by the British, the Americans continued to be victorious.

While wealthy yachtsmen pursued pleasure and fame, thousands of fishermen, with schooners and dories, plied the treacherous waters of the North Atlantic, just to make a living. Schooners from ports including Lunenburg and Gloucester went to the banks—Georges, Quero, and Grand—and the dorymen fished in single or double dories, in bitter cold, sometimes thick-a-fog. They were in pursuit of King Cod, for very little personal gain. Their audience provided not the cheering adulation of spectators, but the quiet, prayerful wishes of families. No journalists recorded their daily moments of danger and hours of backbreaking work. The price of anonymity was high. Conservative estimates for the port of Gloucester show that between eight and ten thousand fishermen lost their lives during the history of the fishing port.

The turn of the twentieth century saw the beginning of an economic boom for Lunenburg. The population numbered a record high of five thousand souls, although many Lunenburgers were fishermen who were gone from the port from April to September. The double dory method of fishing was bringing more money into town for businessmen and captains. Highliner skippers were paid more than ever before. New homes were built, and decorative trim and expansions were added to existing houses.

The Great War, as World War I was called at the time, carried the inflated economic climate along. When the salt fish sales were made in the early months of 1919, fish prices soared to previously unknown heights. Then came the economic crash. The

Canadian wartime fisheries, stimulated by the dramatic reduction of European fishing fleets, ended abruptly. The fishing industry experienced a distinct economic crisis. Families still reeling from the stress and grief of war were now forced to bear the burden of an economic depression.

Lunenburg fishermen were legally regarded as co-adventurers with the owners of the fishing schooners. This meant that they were not guaranteed a set wage, but shared in the profits of the sale of fish. During times of prosperity, the system worked well. During an economic depression, it meant that men might be paid only a few dollars or less after the owners, captains, mates, and cooks had received their share. In addition, the fishermen owed expenses to the companies to pay for their food aboard the schooners. Their families also incurred debts to the company stores.

The worst years for this localized depression were 1919 to 1921, after which conditions gradually improved throughout the 1920s. Many honest fishermen turned to rum-running during this time of prohibition in an attempt to earn a decent wage.

It was during this time of hardship, in the summer of 1920, that the Nova Scotian newspapers began to follow the latest America's Cup race. Sir Thomas Lipton, a wealthy British merchant of tea and grocery fame, was making his fourth attempt to capture the cup for Britain. His yacht, *Shamrock IV*, proved to be his best contender. The series had been postponed for seventeen years, and everyone who had an interest in the sea avidly followed the racing accounts.

Although it proved to be the most exciting series since the inception of the race, it was fraught with delays and problems. At first it seemed that *Shamrock IV* would take the cup, having won the first two races. However, the American *Resolute* came from behind and retained the cup for the New York Yacht Club.

Halifax and Lunenburg businessmen and captains stood back and watched with a palpable feeling of incredulity. The America's Cup races had been postponed several times because of what the yachtsmen had called gales of wind. "Gales!" exploded the Nova Scotians. The gales in which the yachtsmen had refused to sail were just little puffs of breeze, in which North Atlantic dorymen fished every day! The time had come, Nova Scotians sagely agreed, to show the world what a real race was like, between real men.

The Halifax and Lunenburg network worked quickly. The Halifax Herald Limited put up a huge, ornate silver trophy for the new International Fishermen's Series. Led by publisher W. H. Dennis and businessmen H. R. Silver and R. Corbett, among others, a $4,000 purse of prize money was raised for the winner. A $1,000 consolation prize would be given to the loser, to help with expenses.

An invitation was sent to Gloucester. They were told to have an elimination race and send their best schooner to Halifax. There, after the Nova Scotian elimination race, the real race of fishing champions would take place. The basic guidelines stated that the schooners had to have a waterline of 112 feet or less and had to have spent the previous fishing season on the banks. In other words, yachts need not apply.

The excitement poured new vitality into the coastal communities. It seemed that everyone had a favourite schooner or captain, and these races would show the world what they could do. People were also curious to see how the two intrinsically different schooner types would compare: Gloucester vessels were built for speed; Nova Scotian hulls were built to hold as much fish as possible.

When the eliminations were held, Lunenburg's Captain Thomas "Tommy" Himmelman had won the right to represent Nova Scotia aboard his schooner *Delawana*. He had narrowly defeated Captain Angus Walters, whose schooner *Gilbert B. Walters*, named after his two sons, had suffered the loss of the foretopmast during the race. *Alcala*, under Captain Roland Knickle and out of Lunenburg, finished third in the forty-mile race, eight minutes behind *Delawana*. A LaHave ship, *Mona Marie*, finished fifth, while *Independence*, another Lunenburg vessel, finished dead last, thirty-six minutes behind *Delawana*. The one American entrant was Captain Marty Welch's *Esperanto*. Welch had earned the nickname "whitewashed Yankee" when it was revealed that he had been born and raised in the seafaring town of Digby, Nova Scotia.

Delwana and *Esperanto* met at Halifax, in October 1920, full of hope and promise. When the series wrapped up after only two races a feeling of disbelief filled the air: *Esperanto* had won the cup and the prize money. Within weeks, Captain Tommy Himmelman challenged *Esperanto* to another set of races, claiming that he was not satisfied that *Esperanto* was the swifter vessel. The Gloucester committee replied, acknowledged the skill of both vessels, but refused a re-match for that year. Meanwhile, the Nova Scotian organizers were left with the fear that they might have put themselves in the same position as the British contestants for the America's Cup situation. What would they do?

First Elimination Races, 1920. Alcala, Mona Marie, *and* Independence *on the right are seen competing in the elimination races at Halifax. Seven vessels in all took part in the*

elimination races to determine which Canadian vessel would go on to compete against the Americans in the first ever International Fishermen's Series.

What they decided to do was build a new schooner. This would be a vessel that was truly a fishing vessel and would meet all of the physical requirements of the series. The Lunenburg investors, led by Captain Angus J. Walters, H. R. Silver, and the Zwickers of Zwicker and Company Limited, talked with naval architect William J. Roue. He immediately produced plans for a schooner. Unfortunately, the plans would have created a schooner larger than the 112-foot waterline allowed for the series. Mr. Roue was asked to go back to his drawing board.

His next design, based on concepts from his plans for the yacht *Zetes*, was accepted. It was now November 1920 and if this new schooner was to qualify for the 1921 race, construction had to start immediately. The fishing season started in mid-April.

Construction began in December. The Smith and Rhuland Shipyard was alive with workers, and in the moulding loft Richard Smith and George Rhuland transcribed the design from architect's plans to full-sized ribs and planks.

This was the period in which the philosophy of positive thinking became popular. Thousands of people believed and daily repeated the words, "Every day and in every way, I am getting better and better." The shipwrights of Lunenburg lived those words. The new schooner, as yet unnamed, was given a singular honour among Lunenburg vessels. Local politicians had successfully endeavoured to invite the governor general of Canada, the Duke of Devonshire, to perform the driving of the first spike in the keel-laying ceremony.

On December 18, 1920, His Excellency the Governor General of Canada came to Lunenburg. He was later to remark that his visit to Lunenburg was unique within his experience and that he had a great fondness for the schooner that he helped to build.

The governor general arrived in Lunenburg several hours before the ceremony. Politicians and businessmen were delighted to have the opportunity to visit with Lunenburg's most distinguished guest. To break the ice and encourage conversation, a few drinks of fine West Indies rum were consumed. Those drinks were, apparently, followed by a few more. When the time came to go to the shipyard, the community leaders poured themselves into their waiting vehicles and staged an uproariously informal parade through the town's narrow streets.

The ceremony itself was simple. A few words were said, Miss Frances Corkum passed the silver-painted mallet to the governor general, and he swung toward the well-positioned spike. He missed. Taking a slightly tighter grip on the mallet, and peering carefully at the spike, he swung again. He missed again. After a third, equally futile attempt, someone else tapped the spike into place.

It can be safely assumed that the ladies of the WCTU were watching and were not amused. Throughout January and February Angus Walters visited the shipyard every-day. Newspaper articles posted questions regarding the "Great Ark" that was being built, and every plank and piece of oakum was subjected to the scrutiny of the collective wisdom of the town.

This hands-on style of management led to a design change at the behest of Captain Walters. He insisted that the forecastle required more room overhead, as a result of which the bow was raised eighteen inches. The alteration created a distinctive knuck-le in the bow and a unique profile. The change led to a lasting disagreement between the designer and captain; William Roue insisted that it slowed the vessel down, while Angus Walters said it probably helped to give the vessel more speed.

The ship was framed with local spruce and oak and planked with birch, her rails and top were finished in oak, and the deck was covered in pine.

By early March, a name had not yet been chosen for the schooner. Among names offered for consideration was "Cavendish," in honour of Victor Cavendish, the governor general. However, filled with the hope that the vessel would represent Nova Scotia in the International Fishermen's Series, the key organizers chose the name *Bluenose*. Nova Scotians had been called Blue Noses since the 1780s, and it seemed an appropriate name. There had already been at least three Nova Scotian vessels called *Bluenose*, the last having been lost in 1919. The name was popular.

By the middle of March, the initial owners of *Bluenose* formed the Bluenose Schooner Company Limited. Most banks schooners out of Lunenburg were owned by a group of people who had each purchased various numbers of shares that usually added up to sixty-four. The shares would be sold prior to construction in order to cover the cost of building the vessel; each shareholder would in turn receive a percentage of profits after each catch had been sold. According to B. A. Balcom's *History of the Lunenburg Fishing Industry*, this had been the normal arrangement for Lunenburg schooners since the 1880s, but it had a history stretching back to the days of Tudor England.

Since *Bluenose* was going to cost $35,000 to build—double the average cost for a schooner—a different means of financing the venture was required. Thus, it was

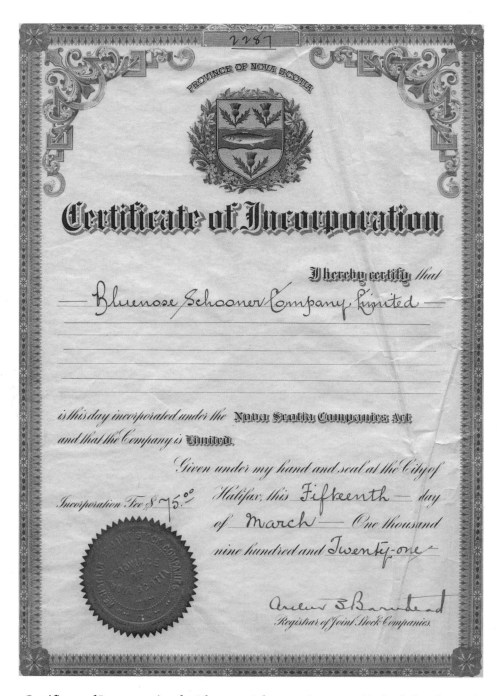

Certificate of Incorporation for Bluenose Schooner Company Limited, dated March 15, 1921. This certificate was part of the Bluenose Schooner Company's minute book. The high cost of Bluenose's construction required a unique financing arrangement.

decided that 350 shares would be sold, rather than the standard 64. Captain Angus Walters took a controlling interest in the company and was appointed managing owner. At the company's meeting of April 12, 1921, the provisional directors resigned, and Angus Walters, Adam Knickle, Hugh R. Silver, Arthur H. Zwicker, and E. Fenwick Zwicker were appointed as directors. Zwicker and Company became the vessel's agent and outfitter and would be responsible for selling the catch.

The involvement of Zwicker and Company connected *Bluenose* to some of Lunenburg's oldest fishing traditions. The company had been founded in 1789, making it the oldest fish company in Canada. Over the course of the nineteenth century, the Zwickers had become active in the West Indies trade, exporting fish products to the Caribbean in exchange for sugar, rum, molasses, and other foods. At one point, Zwicker and Company was the only Lunenburg company with sailing vessels regularly shipping to the West Indies.

The company also pioneered the deep-sea fishing expeditions that established Lunenburg's fishing reputation, when, in 1859, they sent the

Account Ledger for Zwicker and Company. Page 34 of Zwicker and Company's account ledger shows the profits and losses for 1922 for the Bluenose Schooner Company. The price of fish was still healthy when the Bluenose Schooner Company was formed, and the prospects for long-term profits appeared strong. But the late 1920s would be tough years for the fishing industry, and the Great Depression would make the Banks fishery unprofitable.

Bluenose *Launch Day, March 26, 1921. This photograph, by Dewitt Herman, was taken from the harbour looking up onto the launch celebrations with a young Lunenburg boy smiling for the camera. After the celebrations, riggers at the Smith and Rhuland yard quickly completed their work, and by April 15* Bluenose *was ready to go to work.*

schooner *Union* to the Grand Banks. From the company's headquarters at 152 Montague Street, the Zwickers remained some of the most active fish merchants in Nova Scotia for almost two hundred years. The business remained in the Zwicker family until 1977, when it was sold to Deep Sea Trawlers Ltd. The Zwickers were substantial investors in the building of the *Bluenose*. They held a number of outstanding shares in the schooner's original incorporation, outfitted the vessel in 1921, and resold the fish caught off the banks. One of the beauties of the ownership of *Bluenose* was that even small investors were able to participate. Many individuals pooled their money to purchase one share. There were high hopes for the future success of the schooner. These hopes were well founded, as the shareholders went on to recoup their initial investment many times over.

In classic Lunenburg style, people were willing to invest but did not want to tempt fate by making rash statements. No one was better at this than the captain himself. On the day of the launch, as Angus Walters helped to guide the vessel to the Zwicker and Company wharf, a reporter asked him what he thought of the new schooner. "I am delighted with her. She looks everything that she was wanted to look," replied the Lunenburg skipper. "But I'll be able to tell you more about her when I have sailed in her."

STEPPED MATHEMATICALLY PERFECT

2

Eager to conform to the International Fishermen's Series requirement that all vessels participate in a full season of fishing, the Lunenburgers made sure *Bluenose* was read to go to the banks in record time. It required a full community effort. The masts had to be put in place, or as one fellow remarked, they had to be "stepped mathematically perfect." The rigger was Tom Mader, from Mahone Bay. He and his men worked feverishly to get the job done and finished the rigging in five days.

Angus Walters handpicked his crew for the fishing season. It was a typical crew for a Lunenburg schooner. Some of the men were from Newfoundland and others were Nova Scotians. One young lad, Charlie Beck, was seventeen years old. By the standards of the time, he was past his prime for a first-time sailor on a fishing schooner, but Angus Walters asked him to be part of the maiden voyage.

On April 15, 1921, *Bluenose* left Lunenburg, bound for Halifax. On April 16 the vessel set sail for the banks.

Overhauling trawls on a fishing schooner

Bluenose, Canadia, Alcala, *and* Independence, *Halifax Harbour, 1921.* *Four of the eight ships are shown at the beginning of the elimination trials in the fall of 1921. J. Conrad was the captain of Cana-*

Charles Beck was the last surviving member of the maiden voyage, and his memory of the trip remained clear until the end of his days. As he recalled, *Bluenose* was almost lost on that first trip. The vessel was six or seven days out of Halifax, and it was night. Night on the North Atlantic, aboard a two-masted fishing schooner, was a dark and lonely place. The crewmember who was on watch felt the chill air and the rhythmic movements of *Bluenose* on the ocean. Suddenly ahead were the unmistakable glowing lights of a full-rigged ship, coming straight toward *Bluenose.*

dia, Alcala *was under the command of Roland Knickle, and* Independence *was skippered by Albert Himmelman, who had lost the international race the previous year while in command of* Delawana.

The watch rang the bell on the deck of *Bluenose*, but to no avail. The larger vessel did not alter its course. The crewmember rushed down to the after-cabin, where Captain Walters was asleep. The captain was on deck in a flash and gave orders to use the foghorns and bells to make as much noise as possible.

(continued on page 35)

Saltbankers Drying Sails, Lunenburg Harbour. *This Wallace MacAskill photograph shows the Lunen-burg waterfront in all its glory. Thomas Raddall called MacAskill "the poet of the lens" and wrote this about his camera: "The truth is that in his time, and just in his time, he managed to catch various*

aspects of what has been called 'the most beautiful thing ever made by man for a purpose of utility' and in doing so preserved them for posterity."

Elimination Races off Halifax, 1921. *In this photograph of the 1921 elimination race,* Bluenose *(number 2) is off to the right in the lead.* Alcala *is the largest schooner on the left, with number 7 visible*

on its mainsail. Number 5 is Independence, *and* Canadia *is the smallest sail on the right. Wallace MacAskill took this picture while trailing in the vessel on the left.*

Alcala *Racing in the Elimination Trials off Halifax, October, 1921.* Alcala *was a strong contender in the 1921 elimination race, but* Bluenose *demolished all comers. Soon everyone in Nova Scotia was wondering what kind of secret was sailing with the Bluenose. Was it a new design? Did the crew have special sailing skills? Or was Captain Walters the real reason for the schooner's success? The debate would go on for decades.*

(continued from page 29)

Years later, Charles Beck remarked that if anyone had been listening at home in Lunenburg, they would have heard Captain Walters as he added his voice to the cacophonous attempt at signalling. When nothing worked, Angus Walters was left with one remaining command for his crew: "Abandon ship!" In the middle of that inky black April night, all members of the *Bluenose* crew abandoned the vessel in their dories.

Suddenly someone seemed to wake up aboard the other vessel. They altered their course slightly, and the ships passed through the night—"so close," said Charlie, "that you could have thrown a rock from the deck of one and hit the other."

With the disaster averted, the crew rowed their dories back to *Bluenose*, and in the words of Charlie Beck, "it was quite a thrill to get back aboard."

North Atlantic fishermen, especially those from the era of schooners, are masters of understatement. Often they did not tell their families of their narrow escapes from death; incredible feats of courage were described with just a few words, or not at all. In his book *Fisherman of Lunenburg*, James Marsh reports a conversation with an old-timer on the Lunenburg waterfront: "You'd go out in the mornin', waves tall as ships, in a small dory 'bout as big as a rowboat. For hours you'd bob around on the waves, never seein' the main vessel. Wintertime it were severe cold every day. Your face was thick with ice. Your hands froze to your gloves. The winds were always strong. The seas were always high. I lost relatives and friends. You never knew if you were comin' back."

After that inauspicious maiden voyage, *Bluenose* continued on course and proceeded to fish a full season. The first two trips took approximately one month each. By mid-June, the crew had set out again, this time for the full summer. They returned to Lunenburg in early September, at which point vessels were busy unloading their catch and sprucing up for the racing season.

Setting aside the business and practicality of fishing, Nova Scotian schooners met at Halifax for the elimination races. Eight vessels took part in this competition to determine who would challenge the Americans in the second International Fishermen's Series. All eight hailed from Nova Scotia's south shore, including Shelburne, LaHave, and of course Lunenburg. Besides *Bluenose*, the vessels included *Alcala*, *Independence*, *J. Duffy*, *Canadia*, *Ada R. Corkum*, *Donald J. Cook*, and *Delawana*, the previous year's Canadian representative. The crews for the races were handpicked by the captains of

Bluenose *in the Elimination Races, 1921.* *No one was entirely sure why* Bluenose *was so fast, but mos[t] Nova Scotians had an opinion. Richard Smith of the shipbuilding firm Smith and Rhuland offered up h[is]*

view: "I can't tell you what was different from Bluenose *and other ships, and nobody else can. Bill Roue tried to duplicate her lines but he couldn't. She was a good sailor, a big carrier and a great fisherman.*"

the vessels. As a result, each vessel had the full potential to win the race. However, *Bluenose*, with Captain Walters at the helm, would end up the decisive victor.

As the race began, three vessels quickly jumped to the forefront: *Alcala*, *Canadia*, and *Bluenose*. The race had begun in a seven-and-three-quarter-knot breeze, but this soon freshened to twelve knots. By the time the leaders had reached the first mark, the upstart *Bluenose* was in the lead. Fog suddenly came in, making observation from the shore impossible, but by the time the racing schooners had reached the southeast automatic buoy, the fog had lifted, revealing that *Bluenose* had gained a further advantage. As the vessels headed further out towards Sambro Lighthouse, the wind strengthened to twenty knots, and *Bluenose* held its lead. Once the young schooner was able to turn to windward, the contest was over. *Bluenose* rounded the final mark in an easy first place. Captain Angus Walters now knew what he had suspected all summer: *Bluenose* was probably faster than any fishing schooner he had ever sailed.

Having triumphed in the elimination race, *Bluenose* then went on to the second International Fishermen's Series in October 1921. The series was held at Halifax, with the schooner *Elsie* as the American contender. *Esperanto*, winner of the first series, had been lost off Sable Island during the intervening year. The Americans then picked a slinky schooner-yacht called *Mayflower* as their representative. After an editorial in the *Halifax Herald* questioned whether *Mayflower* had had any real fishing experience, the racing committee ruled that the ship was ineligible. In the end, *Elsie*, captained by Marty Welch, was sent to Halifax to defend the trophy.

This series captured the imagination and attention of people all along the Atlantic seaboard. Reporters from both sides of the border covered every aspect of the races. New York newspapers carried reports. In Halifax and Lunenburg, racing "stations" were established. These resembled two parallel clotheslines stretched from one side of the street to the other, with one line holding a small model of *Bluenose* and the other holding a model of *Elsie*. During the races, the models were pushed along the lines when telegraph reports indicated which vessel was in the lead.

As Nova Scotian headlines proudly exclaimed, there was really very little opportunity for "saucy little *Elsie*" to win. *Bluenose* easily won the series and claimed the International Fishermen's Trophy for Canada. *Bluenose* had defeated Elsie in two races. As the wife of one of *Elsie*'s crewmembers stood on a wharf in Halifax, a Nova Scotian offered a few words in conversation. "It's all right, ma'am," he said. "If they hadn't put something in the water today, Elsie would have won." When the woman asked the young man what had been put in the water, he chortled with glee, "*Bluenose!*"

Bluenose *in the Elimination Races, 1921.* *The new vessel* Bluenose *had been given the number 2 for the elimination races of 1921 since it would race against* Delawana, *the previous year's Canadian winner.*

The series against *Elsie* was significant. Not only did it result in a win for Canada, it also put the stamp of good sportsmanship on the contest. During one of the races, *Elsie* lost a portion of sail. It was a moment that would have been seized by most competitors, but Angus Walters opted to take the high road. Looking back at the American schooner, he could see their predicament. He immediately issued orders that the same amount of sail be lowered from *Bluenose*; the vessels were to be evenly matched for the race.

American reporters were astounded by this show of gentlemanly behaviour. New York newspapers recorded the action in detail, commenting that in almost every setting people and teams try to take advantage of any weakness, to win at any cost. The simple race between fishermen was heralded as a significant example of the way in which we should all live and compete.

After the series and the return to Lunenburg, *Bluenose* focused on the business of fishing, continuing to work for the firm of Zwicker and Company. During the winter of 1921–22, *Bluenose* made two trips to Puerto Rico, freighting salt fish. The Gloucestermen, for their part, immediately went looking for a marine architect who could produce a schooner that would outclass the upstart *Bluenose*.

In the meantime, *Bluenose* was embroiled in financial problems. Although the captain, mate, and cook had each been paid handsomely as soon as the vessel had landed in September, the remainder of the crew had had to wait until the fish was sold. By February 1922, the final payments were made.

After these payments were made to the crewmembers and the first dividends were paid out to the shareholders, there was still one outstanding account on the books. W. J. Roue had not yet been paid for his design, although it had been almost a year and a half since he had done the work.

Roue began by gently reminding the Bluenose Schooner Company that he had not been paid. His friend, Halifax businessman H. R. Silver, was the go-between. Silver's first letter on Roue's behalf was dated October 27, 1921. The board of directors eventually met and after due deliberation agreed that Roue had been asked to submit a design, but that he had never been hired by the company or anyone officially representing them. It was therefore the decision of the Company that they did not owe William Roue payment for services that he had, in their opinion, volunteered.

On January 23, 1922, Roue advised the Bluenose Schooner Company that he would be making a sight draft for $884.20, to cover his out-of-pocket expenses during his past visits to Lunenburg and to pay for his fee. On February 2, he wrote to the company to inform them that the sight draft had been returned unaccepted. His patience worn thin, Roue hired the law firm of Murray, MacKinnon and Inglis. The firm wrote to George Rhuland (of the Smith and Rhuland Shipyard) and Captain Angus Walters on February 9, 1922. They sent an additional letter to the Bluenose Schooner Company Limited on February 24, 1922. Their client demanded to be paid.

The owners of *Bluenose* stood firm. They had not, they said, hired Mr. Roue. No contract had been signed. Lunenburg-born H. R. Silver was deeply embarrassed. He was one of the men who had originally talked with Roue about a design for a new vessel. He knew that there had been no binding document, but he felt that it was a matter of honour that some form of payment ought to be offered.

Bluenose *in the Elimination Races, 1922. The photo was taken on the deck of* Bluenose *looking over to* Canadia.
Besides Canadia, Margaret K. Smith *and a newly constructed vessel called* Mahaska *came to Halifax to challenge*
Bluenose *and earn the right to represent Canada in the International Fishermen's Series.* Bluenose *beat all three comers in short order.*

Bluenose *(#1) and* **Henry Ford,** *Gloucester, October 1922.* In the 1922 series Bluenose *beat*
Henry Ford 2–3. *According to G.J. Gillespie in* Bluenose Skipper, *"Despite the clamour of the die-hards*

on the American side of the border, Bluenose *had proved conclusively that she was better than a match for* Ford."

By October 1922, Silver was growing impatient. He declared that if the company did not pay Roue, he himself would pay at least a portion of the alleged bill.

Silver's ultimatum swayed a number of the company's directors. Unwilling to see a well-liked and respected fellow Lunenburger take such a drastic step, they agreed at the meeting of November 25, 1922, to pay Roue $600.

The matter was officially closed, but never forgotten by the participants. With every appearance of eagerness, William Roue strongly supported a Shelburne group in their

Columbia, *"Finest of the American Contenders,"* with Bluenose *in the Background, 1923.*

efforts to build a vessel that could challenge *Bluenose*. The resulting vessel was called *Haligonian* and she would eventually be a major player in the story of *Bluenose*.

In 1922, after a full season of fishing, and while her owners were wrangling over finances, *Bluenose* defeated the other Nova Scotian competitors in the elimination races and sailed to Gloucester to defend her title. To add some glamour to the affair, *Bluenose* arrived at Gloucester under the naval escort of HMCS *Patriot*.

The Americans had worked hard during the winter of 1921–22 to build a ship that could defeat Canada in the series. One contender was supposed to be the schooner *Puritan*, but it followed in the footsteps of *Esperanto*, sinking in June.

After the sinking of *Puritan*, the Americans pinned their hopes on the trim schooner *Henry Ford*. The noted American boatbuilder, Captain Thomas McManus, had been commissioned to build a spirited challenger to *Bluenose*, and had by all accounts succeeded with *Henry Ford*. McManus's vessel had beaten all comers in the American elimination trials and was well commanded under Captain Clayton Morrissey.

Facing off against *Bluenose* in Gloucester, *Henry Ford* took the first race in very little wind, but the results were disqualified because neither schooner had completed the course in the required time limit of six hours. In the second race, *Bluenose* beat *Henry Ford* by nearly eight minutes in a twenty-knot wind. The third race took place in twenty-five-knot winds and saw *Bluenose* again beat *Henry Ford* by eight minutes, capturing the trophy and taking it back to Nova Scotia. Years later *Henry Ford* would fall victim to the so-called curse of American competitors, when the vessel sank near Newfoundland in 1928.

In the 1923 series, *Bluenose* met *Columbia*, the vessel that Captain Walters dignified as the "greatest rival" in the history of *Bluenose*. The vessel had been designed by W. Starling Burgess and launched on April 17, 1923. Called the Gem of the Ocean in Gloucester, *Columbia* beat all contenders in the American elimination trails and arrived in Halifax in October 1923.

In 1923 the great American designer Starling Burgess delivered his best schooner design and the renowned Essex Shipyard launched one of the most beautiful vessels ever built. Her name was *Columbia*, and while she was smaller than *Bluenose*, she was fast.

(continued on page 50)

Captain Walters, Captain Pine, and Crewmembers, Halifax, 1923. *This W.R. MacAskill photo was taken at the A. M. Smith Wharves on the Halifax Waterfront just prior to the start of the first race betwe*

...uenose *and* Columbia. *Captain Angus Walters is sitting in the middle of the picture and Captain Ben*
...ne *is directly above him. The crew of* Columbia *are thought to be the men wearing the ribbons.*

(continued from page 45)

Columbia was skippered by Angus Walters's long-time friend and rival, Captain Ben Pine. Pine was a native Newfoundlander who had immigrated to Gloucester and made a name for himself as a brilliant mariner. Like Captain Walters, Ben Pine was also a shipowner, although he did not sail with any of his schooners to the banks. Captain Pine was actually chief investor in the entire Gloucester fleet but still held his captain's papers and could out-sail just about anyone. He was determined to defeat *Bluenose* and restore American sailing pride.

Upon Pine's arrival in Halifax, Captain Walters had welcomed him and his splendid new vessel: "She looks lovely, Ben," he said, "but she'll have to step lively to beat *Bluenose*." And right at the start *Bluenose* did get a jump on *Columbia*, but the latter would prove an able challenger, one that *Bluenose* couldn't simply sail away from. This time *Bluenose* had a serious competitor and the race would be close.

Bowsprit to bowsprit, the first of three races began neck-and-neck with both sides desperate to establish an advantage of position that would result in extra seconds. Both vessels were bearing down on Bell Rock Buoy, crowding each other and refusing to give up any sea room. At full speed, they collided and their rigging became entangled. *Bluenose* ended up towing *Columbia* for over a minute and a half before breaking free and winning the race by only a little more than a minute. Two fast schooners and two stubborn captains! No official protests were launched since both captains knew that two more races were to come before anyone could claim the trophy.

The second race was held in a twenty-five-mile gale favouring the bigger *Bluenose*, and not surprisingly *Bluenose* took the race. Captain Walters was all smiles when he brought *Bluenose* into the Halifax waterfront. He had won the series against the best vessel the Americans could produce. But Captain Pine lodged an official protest, claiming that *Bluenose* had passed on the wrong side of a buoy. The racing committee awarded the race to *Columbia*, thereby making the series even. Captain Walters could

PREVIOUS PAGE: ***Start of the First** **Bluenose**-Columbia **Race, Halifax, October 27, 1923.*** Bluenose *(#1) and* Columbia *(#2) with their mainsails wide out to catch whatever faint breeze could be had at the start of the race. The starting line was near the Royal Nova Scotia Yacht Club, which is now the site of the container pier next to Point Pleasant Park.*

Bluenose *Leading* **Columbia** *on the Homeward Leg of the Course, 1923.*
Bluenose *is visible in the background of this photo.*

Captains Ben Pine and Angus Walters, Halifax, 1923. *The two friends and fierce rivals are shown here at the height of their careers. After the 1923 Bluenose-Columbia series ended in controversy, the relationship between the two captains was strained until at least 1930.*

Premier E. H. Armstrong Viewing the International Fishermen's Trophy. *Visible behind the trophy in this surreal stereo-photograph, Premier Ernest Armstrong had an international controversy on his hands during those early November days of 1923. He was not a popular premier, having inherited a tired Liberal government that had been in power for over forty years. Armstrong went down in the big Liberal defeat of 1925.*

not contain himself. "Make it no race," he declared. The committee stood firm, the series was now tied one each.

"Come on, boys, we're going home," Walters roared, and even an exasperated Premier E. H. Armstrong could not change his mind. The schooner sailed out of Halifax leaving the racing committee and Captain Pine scratching their heads in disbelief. The Fishermen's International Competition races were over for now. There would be hard feelings and another seven years before Angus Walters and Ben Pine would meet again.

At the November 21, 1923 meeting of the Bluenose Schooner Company Limited, the shareholders approved the conduct of Angus Walters and supported his decision. At the same meeting, the shareholders also broached the subject of selling *Bluenose*. According to the company's minute book, "after some informal discussion as to the advisability of selling the schooner *Bluenose* should a favourable opportunity arise, the meeting adjourned."

At the meeting of December 1, 1923, it was decided that the company was to "forthwith advertise for tenders for the purchase of the schooner *Bluenose*." Ads were to be placed in the Lunenburg, Halifax, Montreal, and Toronto newspapers, and in American papers "if the Managing Director thought fit."

On January 7, 1924, a shareholder named Mr. Covert announced that a Mr. E. C. Adams had made an offer of $18,000 for *Bluenose*. Covert moved that the schooner be sold to Adams and the motion was seconded by H. R. Silver. It is not known what happened with regard to this transaction, as there is no further mention of it in the company's minute book. The original ownership remained intact.

After the racing fiasco of 1923, *Bluenose* did not race internationally for years. But in 1926 a group of Halifax businessmen and Shelburne shipping men commissioned William Roue to design a new vessel that was meant to beat *Bluenose*. The resulting vessel was called *Haligonian*, and it was their dream boat. But the big saltbanker (which was approximately the same size as *Bluenose*) got into considerable trouble fishing off Canso that first summer. The vessel was driven on shore and had to be repaired in time for the October racing season. *Bluenose* had also taken quite a pounding on the sandbars of Sable Island, so both vessels were less than perfect. Captain Moyle Crouse from Lunenburg was at the helm of *Haligonian*. He was an experienced skipper but proved to be no match for Captain Angus Walters. *Bluenose* beat *Haligonian* by sixteen minutes in the first race and also won the second race. Captain Walters

Bluenose Schooner Company Share Certificate. *This certificate is made out to Captain Angus Walters for twenty-one shares at $100 each. Three hundred and fifty shares were issued in total, and while Angus Walters could not claim majority owner with only twenty-one shares, he also had an agreement with the company that as captain and managing owner, he would have complete authority over the affairs of the vessel.*

Haligonian *and* Bluenose, *1926.*

Haligonian *was built to beat* Bluenose, *but she proved to be no match for the Lunenburg vessel.*

Captain Angus Walters at the Wheel, 1936. *This W. R. MacAskill photo shows Captain Walters where he loved to be—at the wheel of* Bluenose.

But back in April of 1926, Angus Walters would have given plenty to be anywhere but behind that wheel.

thought little of this most recent challenger: "Stick a bowsprit in the *Haligonian*'s stern and sail her stern first, she'd do better," was his appraisal.

Bluenose continued to fish in the years after 1923. Perry Conrad made his first trip to sea as the flunky for the 1924 summer crew, sailing from June till September, and his memories capture the lost world of schooner fishing. His father, Albert Conrad, was a dory fisherman in the crew. Twelve-year-old Perry did not receive wages for the trip, but he did earn a bit of money by cutting the tongues and cheeks from some of the fish, salting them, and selling them after they arrived home. Near the end of the trip he also helped Captain Walters with the important job of salting the fish, for which he was given $2. Perry, who went on to become one of Lunenburg's fishing captains, remembered that Captain Walters had been like a father to him. Perry also emphasized Walters's dedication to fishing: "Captain Walters was not just someone with gold braid on his shoulders; he worked. When a load of fish came in, everyone became a deck-hand and so did Angus. He worked. It wasn't just the glory of racing."

Fishing was never a safe occupation, but the years of 1926 and 1927 were especially fraught with disaster on the North Atlantic.

In April 1926, at the start of the fishing season, *Bluenose* limped into port with the loss of two anchors, three hundred fathoms of cable, and a significant loss of fishing gear. Captain Walters reported in the local paper that *Bluenose* had escaped the "worst storm in the history of fishermen." The damage was estimated to be in excess of $2,500. The spring fishing trip was not a success, to say the least.

Before the April storm hit, the fishing had been good off a lee shore near Sable Island. The trawls had been in the water for two days and the dorymen were out, when the temperature plummeted and it began to snow. As the sea began to mount, Captain Walters called the dorymen in. The winds came up, and it appeared that the cable would not hold. *Bluenose* was in only eleven fathoms of water when the seas struck, breaking the cable and smashing over the deck. Sending the men below, Captain Walters lashed himself to the wheel and, with a double-reefed foresail, headed tack for tack into the gale, trying to get around the treacherous sand bars of Sable.

Bluenose survived although two Lunenburg vessels went down that same night. He later recalled that it was his worst night at sea and his mistake had been to anchor so close to danger. But *Bluenose* had held out against hurricane gales. "She never let me down," Walters always said.

Storms or not, the vessels had to keep fishing. Conditions did not improve: two Lunenburg schooners were lost in the gale of August 1926 and four were lost in August 1927.

Although schooner fishing was always an isolating experience, there were sometimes days when vessels would be close enough to "speak" each other, meaning that the captain and possibly other members of the crew would be able to yell and speak to each other. Sometimes they might even go aboard another vessel for a short visit.

During the fine day that preceded the night of the August Gale in 1926, several vessels spoke each other. They caught up on news and inquired whether the other vessels were doing well. Captain John Mosher, of the ill-fated *Sylvia Mosher*, commented that another day or two of fishing would give them a full hold to take home. Without radio receivers, the crews were unaware of the raging hurricane that was headed in their direction.

When night fell and the storm hit, the sense of camaraderie and community was destroyed. Every schooner had to face the towering, sand-filled waves on its own. Every fisherman knew that Sable Island rarely relaxed its hold when vessels fell into its gritty clutches. Once caught in a storm at Sable Island, the only chance that a schooner had was to attempt to cross one of the treacherous shifting sand bars on either end of the tiny island crescent and enter deeper water.

We will never know what the last hours were like for the men who were lost during the gales, but we do have the recollections of the fishermen who were aboard the few vessels that successfully crossed the bar. *Bluenose* was one such vessel. The flunky for the trip was fourteen-year-old Clem Hiltz. Late in life, he could still vividly recall the storm:

> We were fishing at Sable Island, at the bend, for a couple of days, when the storm hit. Angus let out a roar that you could hear a mile away. He lashed himself to the wheel and told everyone to stay down below. Being a good ship and a good captain, that's what saved my life that day.
>
> The men all sat around the galley table and agreed that when the *Bluenose* would strike the bar (when, not if) that they would all go up on deck and hold hands and jump overboard together. That's what they agreed that they would all do. No one would face the last minute alone.
>
> Don't ever let anyone tell you that grown people can't pray, because I heard

them that night. The men sat at the galley table and each man had his dory compass in front of him. And they looked at the compass and kept saying, 'We're not going to survive this.' But we did survive.

Captain Angus Walters was lashed to that wheel for eight hours. He was one of the bravest men who ever sailed the Seven Seas. I owe my life to that man and that good ship. And Angus Walters said that only the *Bluenose* could have survived that Gale, where we were.

August 1927 was marked by another fierce gale. This one claimed four Lunenburg schooners, as well as *Columbia*, *Bluenose*'s old racing rival. In 1929, the Canadian government issued a 50¢ stamp featuring *Bluenose*, with another vessel clearly visible in the background. Captain Walters later declared that he liked to think of the second vessel as *Columbia*, as a tribute to his great rival and fine friends.

A COMMITMENT TO RACING

3

On Saint Patrick's Day of 1930, the Essex shipyard in Massachusetts launched a new vessel, Gertrude L. Thebaud, named after the wife of Louis Thebaud, a wealthy French-Canadian sail-racing fanatic. Captain Ben Pine and Joseph Mellow were the managers. *Gertrude L. Thebaud* was slightly smaller than *Bluenose* and could only carry about eight thousand square feet of sail—one thousand square feet less than *Bluenose.* The American press described her as "light and winsome" and "a sure fire rig."

Eager to compete again against *Bluenose,* Captain Pine and others approached noted racing enthusiast Sir Thomas Lipton—who was well known around the world for his generosity in establishing Lipton Cups for yachting races—and asked that he put up a cup for a special race between *Thebaud* and *Bluenose.* He agreed to put up the cup, with a small amount of prize money.

Ben Pine and Angus Walters had remained close despite their falling-out in 1923. After convincing Lipton to put up the prize, Captain Pine and Gertrude L. Thebaud Inc. issued the challenge to the Bluenose Schooner Company Limited. They proposed that *Bluenose* would meet the just-launched *Thebaud* for a Lipton Cup Series consisting of two races around a double eighteen-mile course near Gloucester. *Bluenose* accepted the challenge.

Gertrude L. Thebaud, *Gloucester, 1930.* *This W.R. MacAskill photograph shows*

Gertrude L. Thebaud *leading* Bluenose *off Gloucester in the race for the Lipton Cup.*

In the interim, *Bluenose* fished the summer season of 1930 under the command of Captain John Walters, brother of Angus. Uncertain while fishing, *Bluenose* went aground on a rock near Burin, Newfoundland, and was stranded for several days. The accident did not help the vessel's nine-year-old hull, but Angus insisted that they would keep their commitment to racing for the Lipton Cup.

In October, with the added indignity of badly stretched sails, a poorly repaired keel, and ballast that had been off-centre for most of the autumn, *Bluenose* arrived in Gloucester to meet *Gertrude L. Thebaud*. *Bluenose* had had ten hard years fishing on the banks, while *Thebaud* was fresh out of the yard. Perhaps unsurprisingly, *Thebaud* won the first race. "We were beaten fair and squarely," said Angus Walters at the finish line. The next day, the American newspaper headlines screamed out the news: "CANADIAN CHAMPION DEFEATED BY AMERICAN!"

The *Bluenose* crew worked all night to tighten the loose sails and right the ballast, but *Bluenose* struggled on the water, and *Thebaud* defeated *Bluenose* in the second race. The new schooner had carried the series. Afterwards, Angus Walters always claimed that he was at fault: "*Thebaud* didn't beat *Bluenose*, she beat me. I didn't use my head!" Following their success in 1930, the Americans were eager to meet *Bluenose* again in 1931. This time they would meet at Halifax and compete for the International Fishermen's Trophy. The great competition was back for the first time since 1923. All Halifax and half of Nova Scotia turned out to see *Thebaud* race against the old queen of the Grand Banks. Angus Walters had insisted on bringing *Bluenose* up to scratch for the series, and her sails were now firm and her ballast balanced. Nevertheless, the bookies down at the old Halifax Hotel on Hollis Street were giving odds on the American challenger.

Much to their surprise—and much to Ben Pine's chagrin—*Bluenose* still had what it takes to win. She won the first race by a whopping thirty-two minutes and the second and deciding race by twelve minutes.

As the victory proved, *Bluenose* might have been an old vessel, but her crew was as dedicated as ever. As G. J. Gillespie put it in *Bluenose Skipper*,

> It didn't matter [that] the paint might be faded and chipped, the dories battered and worn or the one-time white sails a dingy, slaty grey, to them the vessels were living things. As boys who aspire to become doctors and engineers envision gleaming-white surgery theatres or huge bridges with their lattice-works of steel, Angus and his chums had visions too. The inspiration for them came from

the spoon-shaped bows, the decks that creaked underfoot in frosty weather, the patched sails lying furled on the booms or aspread at sea, the hatches, the scuttles and the cabin-houses of the bankers.

After winning the series in Halifax, *Bluenose* returned to Lunenburg and was welcomed by the townsfolk. In his diary entry for Thursday, October 22, 1931, Arthur Risser noted, "Wind North blowing a good breeze. The *Bluenose* arrived home from Halifax at 2. Big time to greet her, but it was soon over, there was a mass of people turned out to welcome her and crew."

Start of the International Schooner Race, Halifax, 1931. *Gertrude L. Thebaud (#2) was the heavy favourite in the 1931 International Fishermen's Series, based on her easy victory the previous year.*

Gertrude L. Thebaud *in Halifax Harbour, 1931.* *The ten-year-old* Bluenose *trounced the much younger* Gertrude L. Thebaud *in 1931.*

The official times for the first race were 5:53:49 for Bluenose *verses 6:26:15 for* Thebaud, *and the second race results were 5:06:12 for* Bluenose *against 5:18:13 for* Thebaud.

"Setting the Fore Topsail." *Life aboard a schooner was hard, but for*

Captain Angus Walters and his crew there were wonderful lessons to be learned from the sea.

With the triumph of 1931, *Bluenose* had once again captured the imagination of the public, and everyone wanted to experience the thrill of sailing on the renowned vessel. This public interest combined with the economically depressed fishery of the 1930s to propel *Bluenose* toward a whole new career.

After the dismal fishing season of 1932, the Bluenose Schooner Company Limited met on March 2, 1933. They decided to form a new company called Lunenburg Exhibitors Limited that would market *Bluenose* as a showboat and travelling tourist attraction. The only other viable option would have been rum-running, which Captain Walters didn't care for.

The shareholders of the Bluenose Schooner Company were permitted to buy one $50 share in the new company for every share that they held in the parent company. The new company printed a small booklet with a history of *Bluenose*, as well as playing cards and a jigsaw puzzle, all of which were to be sold when visiting other ports.

Among the people who sailed on *Bluenose* in these years was Clara Dennis, a Nova Scotia travel writer of the 1930s who produced a two-volume travelogue of the province called *Down in Nova Scotia* and *More about Nova Scotia*. In the latter, she wrote about her thrilling voyage and captured the excitement that many must have felt when they had the chance to set foot on the famous *Bluenose*:

> The *Bluenose* was sailing from Halifax for Lunenburg. I joined her to take the trip. It was grand to be on board the wonder vessel, to be sailing with her to her own home port; the wind in her sails, to see her master-captain, Angus Walters, at the wheel. The *Bluenose*, unchallenged champion of the North Atlantic! She was like some beautiful bird that dips and soars, as she sped through the waves.

In 1933, the first year of her new career, *Bluenose* was invited to represent Canada at the world's fair in Chicago, the Century of Progress Exhibition. Expenses would be

(continued on page 80)

PREVIOUS PAGE: ***Study For Starboard Lookout, 1931.*** *Wallace MacAskill took this photograph off Sable Island aboard a fully-loaded* Bluenose. *With heavy seas all around, MacAskill insisted on being lashed to the pitching, soaking deck so that he could get the exact picture he wanted. Technical knowledge, an artist's eye, and a seaman's courage made MacAskill one of North America's most famous marine photographers.*

Captain Angus Walters With Woman, Possibly Mrs. Elva MacAskill, 1933. *Mrs. Elva MacAskill, whose maiden name was Abriel, was almost as passionate about* Bluenose *and marine photography as her husband. Cruising out of Halifax to Ketch Harbour was their goal most summer weekends, but on most workdays Elva MacAskill could be found in their downtown studio, where she did the hand tinting for their popular series of colour photographs.*

***Crew and Guest on board* Bluenose, *c.1930s.* In the 1930s** Bluenose *reinvented itself*

...nd became a sort of travelling exhibition, charging people for tours and voyages.

Bluenose *in Montreal, 1933.* *On the way to Chicago in 1933, Bluenose pushed up the St. Lawrence, making her first official stop in Montreal. Mayor A. E. Goyette welcomed the popular skipper, his crew, and the most famous celebrity of them all—Bluenose.*

Bluenose *Moored at Dock, Toronto, 1933.* *It cost 25¢ a head for tourists to board* Bluenose, *where they could have their picture taken standing at the wheel of the famous vessel.*

Crew of* Bluenose, *1933. *This MacAskill photograph shows the* Bluenose *crew prior to leaving Lunenburg for the voyage to Chicago. Front row (left to right): Wally Knock, Stewart Walters, and Fred Rhuland; back row (left to right): unidentified, George Whynacht, and Don Bailly. Bailly was the brother of the well-known Lunenburg artist Earl Bailly and Stewart Walters was related to Captain Walters.*

(continued from page 74)

paid, and the *Bluenose* ownership saw potential for making money with daily tours, voyages, and souvenir sales. En route to the exhibition, *Bluenose* did a tour of the St. Lawrence and the Great Lakes, stopping at Montreal and Toronto, among other places. In Chicago, *Bluenose* attracted huge crowds and even won a three-hundred-pound cheese in a race on Lake Michigan.

SCHOONER "BLUENOSE"

HOME PORT—LUNENBURG, NOVA SCOTIA

World's Fastest Sailing Fishing Vessel   Won Four International Races

LAUNCHED AT LUNENBURG, NOVA SCOTIA, MARCH 26, 1921

First Spike driven in her Keel by the Duke of Devonshire, Governor General of Canada

DIMENSIONS

Length - -	143 feet		HEIGHT OF SPARS			
Width - -	27 "	Main Mast -	96 feet	Fore Top Mast	41 feet
Depth of Hole	12 "	Foremast -	86 "	Main Boom -	86 "
Draft of Water	15½ "	Main Top Mast	51 "		

Number of yards of canvas in sails -	21,000 sq. ft.	Numbe. of fish hooks on lines	- -	16,128
Number of feet of rope on boat	- 12,500	Number of boats carried	- - -	8
Length of fishing lines used - -	8 miles	Number of fishermen including captain & cook		21

CARRYING CAPACITY OF FISH, 500,000 LBS.

The Boat fishes on the following Banks:

NEWFOUNDLAND, WESTERN BANK, QUERO BANK AND OTHERS

The "Bluenose" is participating in a Century of Progress, the World's Fair at Chicago, during 1933

LUNENBURG EXHIBITORS LIMITED

LUNENBURG, NOVA SCOTIA

Bluenose *Puzzle Box, 1933. Lunenburg Exhibitors Limited produced a puzzle and a booklet that were sold as souvenirs on the Great Lakes tour. The cover of the puzzle box reads "World's Fastest Sailing Fishing Vessel" in French and English. Cartons of the puzzle were also taken to sell as souvenirs when* Bluenose *went to England in 1935.*

But Depression-era Chicago was also Al Capone country. One night, while docked alongside the Chicago River in a fairly decrepit part of Chicago, gunfire rattled the crewmembers, and before dawn a bullet-riddled body was hauled away. After the exhibition, *Bluenose* returned to Toronto, where the schooner spent the winter before returning to Lunenburg in the spring of 1934.

In November of 1934, the Bluenose Schooner Company Limited decided that they would try to get *Bluenose* to England in 1935 for the Silver Jubilee of King George V. E. Fenwick Zwicker began to contact people in England to see what could be arranged. A contact at a London branch of the Bank of Montreal proved to be the most useful, providing the names of contacts at several yacht clubs and suggesting specific towns and cities with the best harbours. The winter months were spent in a desperate attempt to get funding from private individuals as well as the provincial and federal governments. It was promoted as an opportunity to have Canada officially represented at the Jubilee with the Queen of the North Atlantic.

Artist Earl Bailly with Captain Walters on board* Bluenose, *Chicago, 1933. *Stricken with infantile paralysis when only three years old, the Lunenburg artist Earl Bailly had no use of his arms or legs but managed to learn to write and draw by holding a pencil with his teeth. He eventually became a well-known artist with exhibitions in Halifax, Montreal, Toronto, and New York. He travelled with* Bluenose *to the Chicago World's Fair and was a guest of the Ripley's Believe It or Not exhibition.*

Initially it was proposed that *Gertrude L. Thebaud* would also make the trip, and that there would be an ocean race between the two vessels. However, British clubs would not agree to put up the prize money for the race and the Canadian and American governments were not interested. Ben Pine decided that *Gertrude L. Thebaud* would not make the trip because of probable financial loss.

In March 1935, with almost no funds forthcoming from interested parties on either side of the Atlantic, the directors of the Bluenose Schooner Company decided to finance the trip on their own, if necessary. They made this decision over the objections of most of the shareholders.

Captain George Corkum on the trip to England, 1935. *Despite fourteen years as a hardworking fishing schooner,* Bluenose *sailed from Lunenburg to Plymouth, England, in just seventeen days. Captain Walters and his vessel were received with royal honours.*

Angus Walters Meets King George V, 1935. *Angus Walters onboard the royal yacht* Britannia, *where King George V presented him with a mainsail from the yacht. Although the ailing king had mistakenly referred to* Bluenose *as a herring fisher, in his official remarks he did describe the schooner as "a vessel of considerable merit typical of the spirit of Nova Scotians."*

Bluenose left Nova Scotia for England in early May and arrived late in the month. Upon their arrival, the crew quickly discovered that the souvenirs they had aboard would be heavily taxed to contribute to the Jubilee Fund. But Captain Walters found a way to get around the tax: he decided that all items would be offered as gifts in exchange for "a suitable donation." The "suitable donation," of course, was equivalent to the price of the item. However, Captain Walters also discovered to his dismay that a percentage of all admission fees would have to go to the Jubilee Fund.

Bluenose was the only fishing vessel in the King's Regatta. In a meeting with the King and other members of the Royal Family, Captain Walters was presented with a gift of the mainsail from the royal yacht, *Britannia*. It was given with the understanding that if *Bluenose* was sold to interests outside the banks fisheries, the sails would have to be given to another fishing vessel. It was a tribute to the gallant fishermen of Canada, as much as it was a recognition of the fame of *Bluenose*. Walters was described by the British media as "Captain of the Queen of the North Atlantic."

Unable to resist the attraction to race, *Bluenose* took part in one challenge, a race around the Isle of Wight in July. The sponsor's cost for entering the race was £26. *Bluenose* came third, winning a prize of £25. The outcome was no great surprise, as the other competitors were yachts. Captain Walters was not disappointed: "Sure she beat us," he said, "but even at that the *Bluenose* gave her a run for her money."

While in England, *Bluenose* welcomed thousands of people aboard, and in that sense the trip was a success. But it was not profitable. Captain Walters tried to sell the schooner several times during the visit, but the $20,000 price was too high. The vessel was also chartered for cruises and filmed in a movie about coastal smuggling.

Bluenose left for home in September. Within hours she was caught in such a severe storm that many of the crew despaired of survival. There were also passengers on board, making the trip home. Initially they did not appreciate the danger they were in, and they sat listening to records. As the phonograph played Cole Porter's hit "Anything Goes," one of them asked a crew member if the storm would soon be over. In an effort to prevent panic, he replied with a smooth double-entendre: "Yes," he said, "it will soon be over"—meaning, of course, that soon they would all be dead.

According to Captain Walters, the peak of the storm was reached on September 16. His entry in the log book for that day reads:

> This day begins blowing hard; bad sea running; sky looking very heavy. At 12:30 P.M. reefed jumbo and storm sail. Tied up jumbo at 1:30 P.M. Wind hauled WSW with hurricane force…vessel labouring very hard and terrific sea running…vessel pounding very heavy aft. Impossible to do anything. Continued pouring oil through toilets and by oil bags. At 9 p.m. a terrible sea hit vessel, heaving her on beam ends; breaking foregaff, foreboom, smashing boats…throwing cook stove over on side. Tons of water going below doing other damages, causing vessel to leak very bad. Had to keep continuing pumping…so ends this day.

After the fact, his memories of the storm were just as vivid. "She hit to leeward," he recalled. "It was the biggest sea I ever saw, worse than the night off Sable when we nearly lost ourselves and the vessel. And for the first time in her life the *Bluenose* keeled

Bluenose Survives Hurricane

The following article appeared in "The Western Morning News", a Scottish or English newspaper dated November 19th., 1935. Bluenose reached Plymouth on September 16th., and left for Nova Scotia on October 18th.

SEAMEN SAVED BY LIFELINES

WASHED OVERBOARD IN HURRICANE

FAMOUS SCHOONER REACHES PLYMOUTH

Passengers' Stories Of Ocean Ordeal

SUBMERGED for five minutes, crippled, men manning the pumps washed overboard and buffeted by the tremendous sea, their life-lines holding them to the vessel beneath them — these were some of the amazing incidents in an epic story of the sea, and the triumph of the famous racing schooner Bluenose over the hurricane on Monday night. The vessel limped into Plymouth yesterday morning.

Twenty-one people, ten of whom were passengers in the famous craft looked death in the face at 10 o'clock, when a tremendous sea hit the vessel, which was at that time 200 miles out from Falmouth. She rolled completely to leeward under the tremendous shock, and hundreds of tons of water crashed upon her, flooding her completely.

Down below, five women passengers, who were not allowed on deck, had a few minutes previously started a gramophone record "Anything Goes."

ON BEAM ENDS

Cook's Galley Wrenched Bodily From Deck

Amazing as it may seem, the gramophone, propped securely in a bunk, continued playing but sounding a strident note to the five women who at that moment thought that they were doomed. The vessel stayed in her precarious position for several minutes before she was able to right herself.

Unknown to those below, the crew were waging a desperate battle, and, in fact, two of the members, named Burke and Coolan, were actually overboard, only their life-lines preventing them from being carried away by the terrific seas. These men were amidships, and had been heroically manning the pumps.

When the huge wave hit the craft the cook's galley was wrenched bodily from its holdings, and it crashed across the quarters, doing considerable internal damage to an already badly-crippled vessel.

NO WIRELESS.

Last evening several of the passengers sat around a table at the Continental Hotel at Plymouth dead tired and hardly able to realize that they were alive. One and all were loud in their praise of the conduct of Capt. A. J. Walters and his crew, and also the famous schooner, which had triumphed over tremendous odds.

Without wireless with which to summon assistance she outrode a hurricane. Her captain, who has had 40 years' experience, and encountered some of the worst weather possible, stated to a "Western Morning News" representative, "I have never encountered anything like it."

The passengers were Com. Ian and Mrs. Black, of the Isle of Wight; his sister, Miss Jean Black; Mrs. M. Hamilton Cox, Cowes; Miss Aubrey, Isle of Wight; Mr. and Mrs. Thurburne Helford, near Helston; Mr. B. Gallacher, Cornell University; Mr. P. Aldhan of Windsor Cottage, Castle-hill, Bodmin; and Mr. Frank Humphage, of Bristol.

WOMEN'S PREMONITION

Mrs. Black and Miss Jean Black were asked by "The Western Morning News" representative to tell their story, and it was revealed for the first time that three of them, Mrs. Black, Miss Black, and Miss Aubrey, had a premonition of trouble when they left Falmouth.

"We did not say anything to the others about it not even when Miss Aubrey had a vivid dream," they added.

"I shall never forget the sight that met my eyes when the big wave hit us," said Mrs. Black. "I happened to look along the companionway, and the cook's whole stove was thrown from its fastenings and hurled across the room. How cook was not killed by the impact I do not know.

"We had all assembled in the messroom, giving an eye to the barometer one by one, but each refrained from telling that it was falling rapidly. Jokes, however good, seemed very flat. We had a feeling that we were in for something big.

"Shortly before ten cook came along and gave me a cup of cocoa. We put on a record, "Anything goes," and just at that moment there came a tremendous impact.

WATER IN CABINS

Tons Pour Down Hatchways On Women

"The ship heeled over . . . . heavens, it seemed ages simply ages before she began to right herself, and then it was so slowly that one began to think she would never make it. It was but a matter of four to five minutes, but it seemed like hours. All the time tons of water were pouring down the hatches, and water was already feet deep down below.

"Miss Aubrey was thrown right across the cabin. Her head struck the woodwork with tremendous force, and we thought she was killed. The crack sounded awful in the confined space. It was an hour before she fully recovered her senses, while Mrs. Hamilton Cox sustained a severe blow to her left eye. Curiously enough the gramophone did not stop playing, and I think this fact helped us enormously to recover our fast-fading hopes.

"We would like to mention the bravery of our captain. He was simply splendid, and although in our hearts we knew that he was really worried we admired him tremendously that he could come down to us at intervals, clad in his streaming oilskins, to joke and chat with us, to take our predicament off our minds."

English Newspaper Headlines:
Bluenose *Survives Hurricane, 1935. On the returning voyage across the Atlantic,* Bluenose *met disaster when it ran straight into a hurricane, only 150 miles off the English coast.*

over." The terrible storm tore open the seams, flooding and smashing much of the vessel, but somehow captain and crew were able to right the schooner and pump out tons of water. Defying odds again, *Bluenose* had proven that it could take the very worst punishment the sea had to offer and still stay afloat.

A week later, *Bluenose* limped back to Plymouth for repairs. In late September and early October Angus continually suggested that *Bluenose* should remain in England until the summer of 1936 and that the vessel should be sold while there. The directors agreed that they would sell the vessel if a buyer were found, but insisted that if *Bluenose* remained unsold, it had to return home when repairs were finished. Their final telegram to Captain Walters included the caution that "present war conditions must be taken into consideration" and that it might not be safe for the crew to remain.

Bluenose returned to Lunenburg on November 4. The arrival home was a highlight for the town. According to the diary of Arthur Risser, it was "a beautiful day, warm and sunny, wind light NE mostly calm. *Bluenose* arrived home from the old country. She was away all summer. Bad passage coming home, 23 days."

HARD TIMES

4

After the trip overseas in 1935, Bluenose *experienced some hard times.* The salt fish business was collapsing, and even though Angus Walters had led the fight against the fish dealers to get better prices for the catch, it didn't seem like sailing to the banks was going to be sustainable for much longer. Almost against his will, Angus Walters had allowed engines to be installed in *Bluenose* in 1936 in order that *Bluenose* might get back and forth from the banks fast enough that some of the catch could be sold on the fresh fish market. If the vessel was to be competitive, the change was required. The directors agreed to install two ninety-horsepower Fairbanks-Morse engines. The matter of financing the cash payment of almost $3,500 was left up to Captain Walters.

After several attempts with a number of banks, the Bank of Montreal finally agreed to loan the required money to the company. The loan was personally endorsed by five directors. The Fairbanks-Morse power plant was installed.

Captain Matthew Mitchell, a young lad at the time, was a member of the fishing crew of *Bluenose* in 1936. The crew worked hard, but found Captain Walters to be a fair skipper. They regularly landed their catch at Lockeport, Nova Scotia. Years later Captain Mitchell still recalled one incident from his days on *Bluenose*.

Bluenose *with Captain Walters at the wheel, 1936.* *Clara Dennis took this photograph while sailing on* Bluenose *from Halifax to Lunenburg during the summer of 1936.*

Then I went into the *Bluenose*, me and George Hamilton. We had a chance in the *Bluenose*, whatever time it was in the fall until the next spring. In the *Bluenose* we had a hard breeze of wind one time when I was into her, in fact I believe it was the fourth of February and it was a snowstorm. It was some wind. There must have been probably seventy mile, I would say, up to hurricane force wind and a blinding snowstorm. The wind was northeast and we were laying, I don't know how many days, three or four days for sure. One afternoon somebody happened to be coming back o'er the deck and he said, 'Did you see that vessel?' Nobody seen it. This was the *Keith Collins*. She was laying the same as we were but he gybed her over, putting her on the other tack…that was a close call too. She was right on top of us and we wouldn't have knew it if this guy wouldn't have seen it. He happened to come up from down for'rd and looked to wind'rd and in the snow he seen the black hull. She must have got around far enough that she went clear of us. We weren't doing anything, so we went in Lockeport and George and I pulled out. We left that.

Even in these generally bleak times, *Bluenose* received a national honour. When the new Canadian dime was minted in 1937, *Bluenose* was engraved on the reverse side. The last series took place just one year later and not many Americans were familiar with the new Canadian dime. Crew member Doug Pyke took a bag of Canadian dimes with him to the United States and successfully sold the dimes as "genuine silver engravings of *Bluenose*" for $2 each.

Bluenose was still famous in the late 1930s, thanks in part to the new dime. But she was well past her prime, and few would have taken her for a world-class racing ship.

Passengers on **Bluenose**, *1936. "Why is a vessel called She?" Clara Dennis asked an old seaman during her voyage aboard* Bluenose. *He replied, "The old folks always said that in the days of the square-riggers the first sail was called a skirt and vessels were always she."*

When Captain Ben Pine showed up in Halifax offering to help pay expenses for out-fitting *Bluenose* to race again, Angus Walters was intrigued. He knew that *Bluenose* was in terrible shape but felt it could be fixed up. Captain Pine wanted another go at *Bluenose* while sailing his *Gertrude L. Thebaud*, and the two captains were able to arrange for another race between the two famous vessels. They would meet at Gloucester in October 1938 and compete once again for the International Fishermen's Trophy.

The 1938 series filled the headlines for the entire month of October. In the context of the gloomy 1930s, the series was a welcome reprieve, a reminder of sailing's glory days. And with two old rivals in the race, no one could predict the results.

Crowds at the opening of the International Fishermen's Series, Gloucester, 1938. *Hundreds jammed the waterfron of the historic fishing port of Gloucester to see the old rivals* Bluenose *and* Gertrude L. Thebaud *face off in the revived International Fishermen's Series.*

Bluenose Crew, 1938. Most of Bluenose's crew in 1938 were from Lunenburg or Lunenburg County and were experienced sailors who had crewed on the Bluenose for many years. Claude Darrach, fourth from the left, top row, began working on Bluenose in 1921 and remained with the vessel until the end of 1938. Darrach later became a captain and went on to write his own account of life on Bluenose.

This sense of uncertainty comes through in the diary of Arthur Risser: "Thursday 29 September 1938. Rained last night and cool. Fine today with westerly wind. Bluenose left for USA today for a race next month with schooner Tebeau [sic]. I don't think she can win this time with engines in. They are taken out. She has a challenge."

Another cause for concern among some Lunenburgers was the presence of fifteen-year-old Jean Allen Black on *Bluenose*. A long-standing Lunenburg superstition held that it was unlucky to have a woman aboard a fishing schooner. But that did not prevent Captain Walters from inviting young Jean. Her father, W. Lawrence Allen, was the

(continued on page 98)

Riggers Scramble to Fit a Jib, Halifax, 1938.

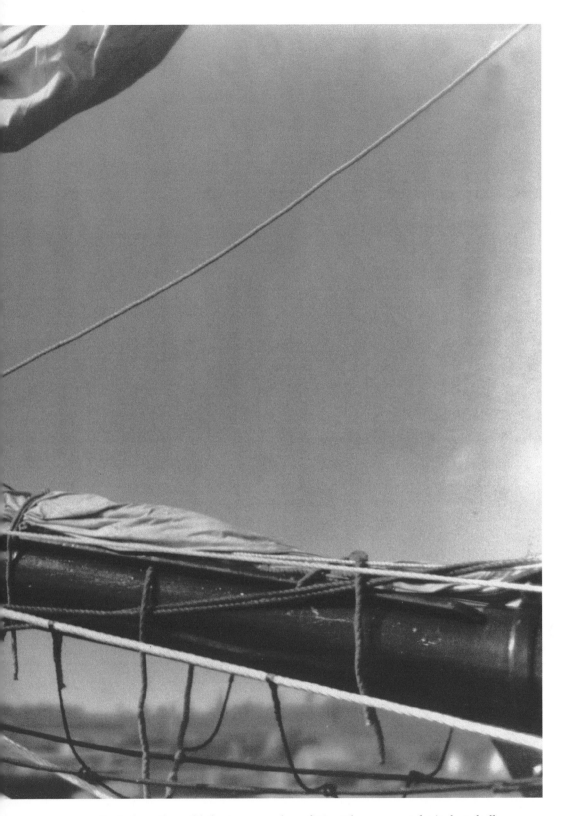

Fresh from the sail loft, riggers are busy fitting Bluenose *out for its last challenger.*

Captain Ben Pine, 1938. *The Newfoundland-born Ben Pine was Bluenose's greatest rival in the International Fishermen's races and skippered the two vessels that competed the hardest against* Bluenose:

Columbia *and* Gertrude L. Thebaud. *This photo was taken in 1938 when Captain Pine's best years as a seafaring captain were behind him.*

Bluenose *at A. M. Smith Wharf, Halifax Waterfront, 1938.* After Bluenose's *victory in 1938, there w*

...ever be another International Fishermen's Series. The age of sailing fishing vessels was coming to an end.

(continued from page 91)

mate aboard *Bluenose* for the last International Fishermen's Series, and she earned the distinction of being one of the few women to ever sail on the original *Bluenose*.

Jean was seasick during most of the voyage, but she still remembers the details of the trip. "Captain Angus was good to me, and so was Doug Pyke. Doug looked after me during some of the rougher moments on deck!" Captain Walters realized that Jean was not feeling well and offered practical advice. "You're seasick, are you?" the skipper asked. He then came back with a piece of salt cod. "Here, chew on this," he said. "You need the salt."

"I don't know if it helped or not," she later commented, "but I chewed it. I felt better later and was able to play cards!"

For a child today, sailing from Nova Scotia to Massachusetts on a fishing schooner would be quite an adventure, but in the context of the 1930s, it was less remarkable. When asked if her classmates were impressed that she had made the trip on *Bluenose*, Black answered, "I don't think that it meant that much to them, really. We all had connections to schooners, back then. It wasn't anything different."

The series was certainly important, however: "While I was there, we went to see as many of the races as we could. There were always crowds of people there for the races. There were a lot of Nova Scotians living in Boston and Gloucester and they were always there. Everyone knew each other."

Unfortunately, Jean could not stay for the entire series: "My grandmother and I returned home before the series finished. I had to get back to school."

What happened in the series is now legendary—the tense five races, the stunning victory by *Bluenose*, the jubilant crowds. Battered and tired though the schooner was, *Bluenose* proved that it still had what it took to win. It was a fitting end to the age of sail.

A SAILING AMBASSADOR

5

The year of his triumph in the last International Fishermen's Series was also a year of personal change for Captain Angus Walters, who was usually reticent when it came to talking about his personal life.

In 1937, after twenty-nine years of marriage, his wife Maggie passed away. Their three sons, Gilbert, Bernard, and Stewart, were deeply saddened by their loss. Their mother had provided a constant foundation for the family, especially during times when Angus was away. The master of *Bluenose* was no less adrift in his grief.

However, hope springs eternal and within a matter of months, Angus met the young and lovely Mildred Butler in Halifax. At first the almost thirty-year difference in their ages meant that they were mere acquaintances. Mildred was a waitress in a Halifax restaurant, and Angus would stop there when he was in the city.

During the first half of 1938 they quietly realized that their friendship had deepened into love. They agreed to keep their relationship private, but in the heat of the month-long separation during the October 1938 series, Angus announced that he would be flying home to Nova Scotia when the series ended, to join his fiancée.

The wire services quickly picked up on the story and reporters were soon knocking on Mildred's door. She refused to speak with them until she was shown published proof that Angus had "spilled the beans." Then, with a relaxed laugh and a flash of dimples, she shyly confirmed that they were engaged. She also noted that since she suffered from seasickness, she doubted that they would be travelling far aboard *Bluenose*.

The press and the public loved it. Enchanting photographs of the bride-to-be appeared in newspapers in Canada and the United States.

They were married in December and resided in Halifax for several months. Angus had many friends in the city, but his heart was on the south shore. They moved to Lunenburg in 1939 and made the best of a sometimes difficult situation. Gossip was sometimes harsh with regard to the difference in their ages. The most unsettling aspect, however, was the reception that certain members of the Walters family reserved for the new bride. Feeling that his father had married too soon after the death of his mother, Angus's son Bernard referred to Mildred as "that woman" for the rest of his life.

By all accounts, Angus and Mildred loved each other throughout their marriage. Their happiness was cut short in 1957 when Mildred succumbed to cancer. Angus did not remarry, although he apparently did not lack for female companionship.

NEARING THE END

Meanwhile, the future of *Bluenose* was an open question. The prospects for fishing had not improved, and the vessel was not getting any younger. At a meeting of the Lunenburg Town Council on November 14, 1938, it was proposed that a commission be formed to purchase *Bluenose* and provide a fund to keep the vessel in repair.
E. F. Zwicker sent a letter to the mayor, Arthur Schwartz, on November 16:

> Moyle Smith and Adam Knickle resolved that this Board [Bluenose Schooner Company Limited] agree to sell the schooner Bluenose to a proposed Commission of which Mayor Arthur Schwartz of Lunenburg, Nova Scotia, is to be chairman for the sum of $20,000.00, this price to include engines and all equipment with the exception of fishing gear with the understanding that she remains under the management of said Commission and with the further understanding that Captain Angus Walters is to have the option of accepting the position of caretaker of the vessel. This offer is subject to acceptance within 30 days.

Saves Bluenose

Cap'n Angus Pays $7000 One Hour Before Auction

THE BLUENOSE

LUNENBURG, Nov. 14.—Captain Angus Walters came to the rescue of the Bluenose today when he placed $7000 on the Sheriff's desk one hour before the Queen of the North Atlantic fishing fleet was to be auctioned. Sale of the schooner had been ordered by the courts in an action for debt, at the suit of the Canadian Fairbanks Morse Co. Ltd., whose claim was for the amount of $7000 the balance due on the cost of engines installed in the schooner three years ago.

Capt. Walters said: "I would not see the schooner sold which so faithfully served me, the town of Lunenburg and the owners for over 18 years." The Bluenose is still owned by the Bluenose Schooner Company of which Zwicker and Company are the chief shareholders.

"I have faith in the Bluenose and will have for some time to come and I think it a disgrace the schooner should have been threatened with the auction block. I still will protect the Bluenose with all I have as she served me too faithfully to be let down," Capt. Walters declared.

He said the Bluenose may go fishing in the Spring and added the plan originated by

CAPT. ANGUS WALTERS

a committee of public spirited men in Lunenburg to take over the Bluenose and preserve her as a memorial had fallen through.

Saves Bluenose *One Hour Before Auction,* **Halifax Herald,** *November 14, 1939.* Captain Walters's costly effort to save Bluenose *showed just how much the old vessel meant to him.*

***Marine Survey of* Bluenose, Lunenburg, 1940.** *Wallace MacAskill is thought to have undertaken an extensive photographic survey of* Bluenose *around 1940 to determine the vessel's value, and what was revealed was not encouraging. The* Bluenose *was in rough shape after almost twenty years at sea.*

The town, in turn, requested an extension of six months. The company agreed to an extension till noon on February 15, 1939, on the condition that a preliminary payment of $2,000 would be made by December 20. The resulting commission was called the Committee for the Preservation of the Schooner Bluenose. When it became apparent that money was not forthcoming, the deadline for payment was extended again, to April 1, 1939. But that deadline was also broken, and the plan never came to fruition. The funds were simply not available from the townspeople on the brink of war. As a last-ditch effort, they launched a Canada-wide campaign for school children and others to send in dimes to save *Bluenose*, but that too failed to raise enough money.

***Marine Survey of* Bluenose*, Lunenburg, 1940** . *The sale of* Bluenose *in 1942 was a sad day for Lunenburg.Here we can see the aged vessel docked at Lunenburg, looking out into the harbour, port side to midship.*

Adding to *Bluenose*'s problems, the Fairbanks-Morse engines that had been installed in 1936 had still not been paid for by the summer of 1939. The company declared that fishing had been so poor that they did not have the money to pay for them. On September 12, 1939, after several warnings, Fairbanks-Morse issued a writ to the Bluenose Schooner Company Limited. The amount owed was $7,200.

On November 7, there was a special meeting of the shareholders of the Bluenose Schooner Company Limited. Senator Duff requested information regarding this matter and expressed the view that the meeting should censure the board of directors for

Captain Angus Walters, 1961*. Angus Walters was born on June 9, 1881, and died August 12, 1968, having dedicated much of his life to* Bluenose. *As an old man, he often reminisced about his years as captain of the famous ship.*

its financial profligacy. Over the years the shareholders had seen dividends equivalent to almost 150 per cent of their original investment.

Senator Duff proposed that a committee of three meet to discuss the matter with Fairbanks-Morse. The committee was comprised of W. H. Smith, Senator Duff, and Wallace Knock. Fairbanks-Morse, having patiently waited for years for the remainder of their funds, continued with the legal proceedings. *Bluenose* was scheduled to go up on auction at a sheriff's sale within days. On November 14, one hour before the auction was to begin, Angus Walters informed the board that Fairbanks-Morse was willing to accept $7000 as complete settlement, and that Captain Walters and his sons had arranged for this amount. The Walters family had rescued the vessel from the shame of a public auction, at considerable personal financial sacrifice. "I would not see the schooner sold which so faithfully served me, the town of Lunenburg and the owners for over eighteen years," Captain Walters explained.

In January, Captain Walters said that he would not send *Bluenose* fishing in 1940. She had been spared the indignity of a sheriff's auction, but *Bluenose* would still have to be sold, albeit in a less humiliating fashion. Ads announcing the sale were placed in the Halifax papers during the week of January 15. Although there were several interested buyers, the company could not reach an agreement on any of the offers. In the end, Angus Walters himself ended up buying the vessel, when the company accepted his offer of $10,000. The master of the vessel had become owner.

By 1941 wartime conditions were grim. Fishing schooners were in danger of German U-boat attacks; they were also sometimes cut down when caught in the way of convoys to Europe. Fish prices were not favourable.

Although Angus Walters had saved *Bluenose* the previous year, it was only a delaying tactic. During World War II, only a rich man could afford to keep a large schooner that was not bringing in any money. With much regret, the captain realized that he could not continue to keep the vessel afloat by himself, even with the help of his sons. He decided to sell *Bluenose* in late 1941. On January 3, 1942, Jesse Spalding III and Sanford Johnson, both Americans, paid $20,000 for *Bluenose*. They also bought the schooner *Kaymarie*.

They set up in Halifax and formed the West Indies Trading Company to own and operate the two vessels as freighters in the Caribbean. With spars cut down to a lower height, and with various pieces of memorabilia left behind, *Bluenose* left Lunenburg harbour for the last time and went to Havana, Cuba. According to Spalding, *Bluenose* was recognized as a famous schooner from the moment she arrived in Cuba.

The first scheduled run of *Bluenose* for this company was between Port Everglades and Havana with 140 tons of dynamite and 60 tons of caps. The crew included many Nova Scotians, notably the captain, Wilson Berringer. During the war *Bluenose* worked for the United States War Shipping Administration, joining many other older fishing schooners in the work of freighting supplies.

It was during one such run, late at night, that *Bluenose* encountered a German U-boat. At about 2 A.M., in the dark, the submarine surfaced. The hatch of the coning tower opened and an officer, using a speaking trumpet, called out to the vessel. "What," he asked in perfect Oxbridge English, "are you doing here?" One of the crew called back, "Fishing—what else?"

The officer's reply was swift and pithy. "I know what you are doing. You are the *Bluenose* and if I did not love that vessel so much, I would blow you out of the water now. Get the hell to shore and don't come back. Next time you will not be so lucky."

Jesse Spalding claimed that *Bluenose* grossed $500,000 for him, running trips back and forth to the United States. But with the end of the war and its guaranteed profits, the West Indies Trading Company decided to sell *Bluenose* to the New York–based firm of Farr and Company. Shortly thereafter, in January 1946, *Bluenose* went aground on a reef near Haiti. Lunenburgers received word that the vessel's back was broken, the keel beyond repair. Within days the vessel sank. Headlines across Canada shouted that it was a "National Disgrace." The only consolation was that no human lives were lost.

No one felt the loss of *Bluenose* more keenly than Captain Angus Walters, who was curling at the Lunenburg Curling Club when he heard the news. His son Bernard later said that Captain Walters cried for hours.

Captain Walters wrote to government officials in Haiti to see if there was an opportunity for a salvage operation. He received respectful replies, all stating that *Bluenose* was truly gone forever.

However, memories of *Bluenose* did not die. With the passage of years, journalists, enthusiasts, and everyday folks made the trip to Lunenburg to talk with Captain Walters. He had started a new business in the early 1940s, the Lunenburg Dairy, which saw him getting up every morning by 5 A.M. and overseeing the collection and pasteurization of milk, as well as the delivery. He welcomed any visitor who came to share memories and to talk about *Bluenose*.

The importance of *Bluenose* to Lunenburgers is exemplified by the late Fred Spindler, who was five years old when *Bluenose* was launched, and who loved to share his memories of the vessel. All his life, his childhood memories of the vessel were as clear as the twinkle in his eyes.

"It was the largest crowd of people that I had ever seen," he said of the launch. "My mother took me to the top of Blockhouse Hill and we watched the launching. I asked her why there were so many people; she told me that the *Bluenose* was a special vessel, being built for racing."

When Fred returned home, his mother wrote the name *Bluenose* on his blackboard. Fred neatly printed the name beneath it and knew that this was something very special.

Young Fred was like all of the youngsters in Lunenburg. They eagerly followed the career of *Bluenose*. "I remember the lines, like clothes-lines, that were suspended above Lincoln Street, between G. A. Silver's and what became Knickle's Studio. For the first race, a model of *Bluenose* was attached to one line. A model of the American schooner *Elsie* was attached to the other. We would run out of school and down the hill to see how the race was going. The models were moved along the lines, as telegrams were received to tell us the details of each race."

The exploits of Captain Angus Walters and *Bluenose* were often discussed in the Spindler household. Fred's father was Captain Willet Spindler; his mother's name was Loretta. Fishing was a way of life for the family, with Captain Spindler away on fishing schooners for long periods of time. One of his vessels was *Lauretta Frances*, named for Fred's mother. In good Lunenburg fashion, Captain Spindler spelled the name of the vessel Lauretta, rather than Loretta, in order to have three A's in the name for good luck.

As he grew up, Fred continued to have a strong interest in *Bluenose*. When the last International Fishermen's Series was held in 1938, Fred was a student at Mount Allison University, where he played on the university football team. On the day of the deciding race, Fred was out on a practice with the team. Suddenly one of the students from his residence called to him: "Spindler! *Bluenose* won!" Everyone cheered.

In 1941, Fred joined the Navy. The first three months of 1942 were spent in training, near Victoria, British Columbia. One evening Fred and a friend were invited to someone's home for dinner. The hosts politely inquired where the two men were from.

(continued on page 113)

Bluenose II *under construction, 1963.* *Designed to be a full size replica of the original* Bluenose *that would be a sailing ambassador for Nova Scotia and Canada,* Bluenose II *was built at the same Smith and Rhuland Shipyard that had constructed* Bluenose *back in 1921*

Driving the first spike in the keel of* Bluenose II, *February 27, 1963. *Captain Walters drives the ceremonial "golden" spike at the keel laying of* Bluenose II *in Lunenburg. William Roue, designer of the original* Bluenose, *stands directly behind him. In the back row, left to right, stand Victor Oland, Fred Rhuland, and Colonel Sidney Oland.*

Launch of Bluenose II, *Lunenburg, July 23, 1963.*

Nova Scotia's seafaring heritage got an enormous boost in 1963 with the launch of the replica schooner Bluenose II.

Bluenose II, *July 1969*

(continued on page 107)

Fred's friend, from Amherst, Nova Scotia, replied first. The hosts had never heard of Amherst. They then asked Fred the name of his home and he replied, "Lunenburg, Nova Scotia." As Mr. Spindler remembers it, "They knew all about Lunenburg and they knew about *Bluenose. Bluenose* helped to put Lunenburg on the map!"

Fred was back in Lunenburg when *Bluenose* was lost. In fact he was in the Lunenburg Curling Club on that fateful night in January 1946, along with Captain Angus Walters.

His voice dropped to low tones when he recalled that time: "I answered the telephone. It was one of the Halifax newspapers and they wanted to speak with Captain Angus Walters. They had tracked him down to the Curling Club. It was quite a shock to all of us; it was the first that we had heard the news."

Given the strong feelings that many still had for *Bluenose*, it is hardly surprising that an effort would be made to bring the schooner back to life. In 1960 a replica of the famous *HMS Bounty* was built at the Smith and Rhuland Shipyard in Lunenburg for the MGM movie *Mutiny on the Bounty*. Thousands of visitors came to town for the launch of the vessel. Lunenburgers, especially Captain Walters, were inspired. If they could build a replica of *Bounty*, surely they could do the same for *Bluenose*.

The Oland family came to the forefront. Wealthy and known for their production of ale—including, appropriately enough, Schooner Beer—they agreed to finance the reconstruction. While the original *Bluenose* had cost $35,000 in 1921, forty-two years later, *Bluenose II* cost $300,000.

In July 1963, *Bluenose II* slid down the ways at the Smith and Rhuland Shipyard. Many of the men who had worked on the original vessel were involved in the construction of the new schooner. Angus Walters and the designer, William Roue, were both on hand, every step of the way.

At the launch, Captain Walters received a commemorative certificate that appointed him honorary captain of the ship "in recognition of the special and lasting place which the immortal *Bluenose*, undefeated and International Sailing Champion and Queen of the Seas, carved for herself in the hearts of Canadians through her exploits and triumphs under the hand of her Master-Mariner."

There has been no other subject that has captured the hearts and minds of Lunen-burgers as much as the stories associated with the original *Bluenose* and its captain, Angus Walters. People of all ages look to *Bluenose* as a reflection of glorious times past, to the best of our age of sail, to spirit and adventure. A sprightly and determined captain, the many brave crewmembers, and a dark-hulled beauty—Queen of the Grand Banks—have established themselves as a part of the town's maritime heritage, a heritage that is at once both vibrantly alive and yet part of a distinctly different age.

The fascination with *Bluenose*, however, is not confined to the town of Lunenburg. The memory of *Bluenose* is alive in countries around the world. For some people, it might only be the name. They have heard of *Bluenose*, but they do not know what it means. For many others, *Bluenose* personifies grace, courage, and victory.

In the 1990s, history came full circle and Captain Wayne Walters, a grandson of Angus Walters, became master of *Bluenose II*. At that time, a woman from Norway went on one of the two-hour cruises offered by the new vessel.

An older woman, she had lived through the German occupation of her country during the Second World War. In her purse, she had a faded and well-folded newspaper clipping. It was from a Norwegian newspaper during the war. She wanted to explain to the crew of *Bluenose II* what *Bluenose* had meant to her family and to their friends. The clipping was a story about *Bluenose* and was written from the point of view of the brave vessel beating all odds and winning the last International Series in 1938. The story was a retrospective, written several years after the series.

The Norwegian woman explained that in the dark days of the war, any story of hope was eagerly embraced. Her family had carefully cut the clipping from the newspaper and, when it seemed that their country might never come out of the occupation, they shared the story of *Bluenose*'s inspiring victory. It brought them hope, and the clipping itself became a cherished heirloom.

It was her desire to visit Nova Scotia, while she still could, and sail aboard *Bluenose II*. She wanted to pay tribute and give thanks to the original vessel that had brought light to their lives during their darkest hours.

The original vessel and its gallant captain may no longer be with us, but as long as there is a maritime memory, *Bluenose* will never die.

APPENDIX

CAPTAIN WALTERS SPEAKS

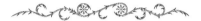

In 1963, the Historic Sites and Monuments Board of Canada unveiled a plaque in Lunenburg, recognizing *Bluenose* as a symbol of national historic significance. This prompted Angus Walters to write a letter about his memories of *Bluenose*. It was first published in *The Chronicle Herald* on June 16, 1953.

> Sir, for the information of Mayor Zwicker, of Lunenburg, and other citizens who may have attended the unveiling of the Bluenose plaque the other day, I would like to present the facts about the famous schooner.
>
> Actually, no one in Lunenburg was responsible for having her built. The credit goes to a group of Halifax businessmen including H. R. Silver, the Hon. W. H. Dennis, the late Reg Corbett and the late Harry DeWolfe. In 1920, these men got in touch with some of us in Lunenburg to see if a fishermen's race could be held off Halifax Harbour. Arrangements were quickly made and the race was held, with Delawana being the winner [of the Nova Scotian elimination race].
>
> Then, the Halifax men decided they would like to have an international race and they invited the Gloucestermen to take part. Vessels came down and the race was won by Esperanto of Gloucester.

Naturally, everybody wanted the honor and The Halifax Herald Trophy to come back to Nova Scotia and so the same group of men made inquiries about having a schooner built. At that time they came to me and asked me to go to Halifax to talk matters over with them and to become the vessel's skipper. I refused at first because I had a new vessel, the Gilbert B. Walters and was satisfied, but at length they prevailed.

We held the conference in Halifax and they introduced me to W. J. Roue, the designer. From the very first I insisted that I have the controlling interest in the vessel, and here I would like to say that Bluenose was not only a racer, but she was a worker. She paid back every dollar that was put into her and with good interest too.

The races were held and as everyone knows, Bluenose was the winner, proving the best of them all, time after time. I don't know why the Halifax men wanted me to be skipper in the first place, but I do know that the full honor for the victories should go to Bluenose herself and to the gallant men who served as her crew.

When the racing was over, the Bluenose went to work and earned her keep, but eventually, when engines were put in, I had to put up the 7200 dollars to keep her from going on the auction block. None of the other owners who were Lunenburg men offered any help at that time.

Later on, the vessel was offered to them, as Mayor Zwicker can recall, but they would not purchase it from the Bluenose Schooner Company Limited, of which I was the majority owner, and again I had to stake what I had to buy her. I was glad I did so because I think I saved her then.

Eventually, when the war began in 1939 and I was in another business, she was tied up. Efforts were made to sell her to the provincial government because she had brought so much fame to Nova Scotia and they failed, and again no one in Lunenburg offered to take her off my hands. I had to sell her and she was disposed of in the West Indies to which she had taken a cargo of fish.

I did not want to sell her, but circumstances compelled me to do so and I feel to the shame of the province and the Town of Lunenburg, and citizens who were in a position to have set up the Bluenose as a permanent memorial of a fast-dying way of fishing, that she was allowed to go south to flounder and rest on a bed of rocks.